The Genius of Money

Mark,

Thanks for being a
pioneer and mentor in
this space
It is highly appreciated

Brigitte

The Genius of Money

Essays and Interviews
Reimagining the Financial World

John Bloom

2009 SteinerBooks

The following credits are gratefully acknowledged:

p. 2. *The Tribute Money*, Masaccio (Maso di San Giovanni) (c. 1401-1428). Fresco, c. 1425. Brancacci Chapel, S. Maria del Carmine, Florence, Italy. Photo credit: Scala/Art Resource, NY.

p. 5. *The Tribute Money: Christ and the Pharisee*, Titian (Tiziano Vecellio) (c. 1488-1576). Gemaeldegalerie Atle Meister, Staatliche Kunstsammlungen, Dresden, Germany. Photo credit: Erich Lessing/Art Resource, NY.

p. 6. "Deciding," from *An Oregon Message*, William Stafford (1914-1993), Harper & Row, 1987.

p. 8. *Danae and the Shower of Gold*, Titian (Tiziano Vecellio) (c. 1488-1576). Oil on Canvas, 1553-1554. Museo del Prado, Madrid, Spain. Photo credit: Scala/Art Resource, NY.

p. 12. *Barrels of Money*, Victor Dubreuil (1880-1910). Oil on canvas, c. 1898. Board of Governors of the Federal Reserve System, Washington, D.C. Purchased with funds from Bartel Zachry, G. William Miller, John Wieland, John Whitehead, Russell Family and Foundation, Carolyn Chambers, Robert Erburu, Richard Kelly, Gary Michael, John N. Nordstrom, Susan Phillips, Michael Sonnenreich, Roselyne Swig, Ronald Abramson, Alsdorf Foundation, Huntington T. Block, Therese Harris, Gerald D. Hines, Thelma and Melvin Lenkin Family Foundation, Michele Smith, and Bernard Osher, and from general acquisition funds, 2004.

p. 24. *The Money Lender and His Wife*, Quentin Metsys (c. 1446-1530). Oil on wood, 1514. Photo by Gerard Blot. Louvre, Paris, France. Photo credit: Reunion des Musees Nationaux/Art Resource, NY.

p. 28. *Beggars at the Door*, Rembrandt van Rijn (1606-1669). Engraving, 1648. Photo credit: Rijksmuseum, Amsterdam.

p. 30. *The Seven Works of Charity*, Feeding the Hungry, Master of Alkmaar (1490-1510). Panel of a polyptych, 1504. Photo credit: Rijksmuseum, Amsterdam.

p. 34. *The Payment of Taxes*, Georges de La Tour (1593-1652). Ca. 1618-1620. Art Gallery, Lviv (Lwow), Ukraine. Photo credit: Erich Lessing/Art Resource, NY.

p. 38. *The Rich Man*, Hans Holbein the Younger (1497-1543). Proof print before 1526, first published 1538. From the series Dance of Death. British Museum, London, Great Britain. Photo credit: Copyright The Trustees of The British Museum/Art Resource, NY.

p. 40. *Usurer with a Tearful Woman*, Gabriel Metsu (1629-1667). Oil on canvas, 1654. Museum of Fine Arts, Boston Sidney Bartlett Bequest 89.501. Photo credit: Copyright 2009 Museum of Fine Arts, Boston.

p. 44. *Judas Receiving Payment for His Betrayal*, Giotto di Bondone (1266-1336). Fresco, 1304-1306. Scrovegni Chapel, Padua, Italy. Photo credit: Alinari/Art Resource, NY.

p. 46. *Ten Dollar Bill*, Roy Lichtenstein (1923-1997). Lithograph, 1956. Photo credit: Copyright Estate of Roy Lichtenstein, 2009.

p. 48. *Front and Back Dollar Bills*, Andy Warhol (1928-1987). Synthetic polymer paint and silkscreen ink on canvas, 1962. Copyright The Andy Warhol Foundation for the Visual Arts/ARS, NY. Photo credit: The Andy Warhol Foundation, Inc./Art Resource, NY.

p. 53. J. S. G. Boggs Bill. From *Boggs: A Comedy of Values* by Lawrence Weschler, The University of Chicago Press, 1999. Courtesy of the artist.

p. 59. The Labyrinth at Lifebridge Sanctuary, New York. Photo by the author.

p. 71. "Economics and the Presence of Philanthropy" reprinted with permission of onPhilanthropy (www.onphilanthropy.com) published by CauseWired Communications.

p. 76. *Wall Street, 1915*, Paul Strand (1890-1976). Platinum print photograph. Copyright Aperture Foundation. Philadelphia Museum of Art, Philadelphia, Pennsylvania, U.S.A. Gift of the Estate of Paul Strand, 1980. Photo credit: The Philadelphia Museum of Art/Art Resource, NY.

Published by SteinerBooks
610 Main Street, Great Barrington, Massachusetts 01230
www.steinerbooks.org

Library of Congress Cataloging-in-Publication Data

Bloom, John.
  The genius of money : essays and interviews reimagining the
financial world / John Bloom.
      p. cm.
  ISBN: 978-0-88010-634-4
  1. Money. 2. Finances I. Title.
  HG221.B5742 2009
  332.4—dc22
                                                    2009028373

Printed in the United States of America

Acknowledgments

No work such as this collection of writing is possible without a great deal of support invisible to the reader—and sometimes to the writer. Inspiration, inquiry, and insight were my greatest accomplices in giving language to thought and form to ideas. Love, patience, interest, and encouragement from family and colleagues were powerful motivators for tackling even a portion of such an all-encompassing topic as money. I would like to thank RSF Social Finance for supporting me as a member of its staff in my inquiry about money and for supporting this publication. RSF's financial and social mission in investing, lending, and giving, and its roots in the work of Rudolf Steiner are a living laboratory into money and its uses. Finally, the time to gestate this book, particularly over the last three years, was made possible by the support of the AnJel Fund at RSF. This kind of generosity, one that recognizes unfolding destiny paths, is profoundly energizing and humbling, and a true gift-blessing, which I hope this book honors.

Contents

INTRODUCTION: Money Being Transformed   XI

PART I
THE POETICS OF MONEY

1. Tribute Paid: At the Intersection of Spirit and Money   3
2. Coining a Myth: Titian—*Danae and the Shower of Gold*   9
3. Trumped Money: Value and the Eye of the Beholder   13
4. The Other Invisible Hand: Money and Its Subtle Influence
    on Social Life   15
5. Reforging Adam Smith: Beyond the Gates of Self-Interest   19
6. An Inventory of Polarities: Quentin Metsys—*The Money Lender
    and His Wife*   25
7. Begging to Differ: Charity at the Threshold   29
8. Economic Chiaroscuro: Georges de La Tour—*The Payment of Taxes*   35
9. Money and the Dance of Death: Hans Holbein the Younger—
    The Rich Man   38
10. Mercy in Mercantile Times: Gabriel Metsu—*Usurer with
    Tearful Woman*   41
11. Judas's Dilemma, Giotto's Rendition   43
12. Free Market Money in a Pop Iconomy   47
13. Money and the Modern Mind   51
14. The Touchstone and the Labyrinth: A Step into the Mystery
    of Money   57
15. The Transcendentalist and the Immigrant: Two Views of Money
    in America   63

PART II
A TOPOGRAPHY OF TRANSACTIONS

1. Economics and the Presence of Philanthropy 71
2. A Window into Transparency: The Desire for Connection through Finance 74
3. Just Money and Social Finance 80
4. Consuming Identity 84
5. Real Virtuality: QQ Coins and the Quandary of Complementary Mercantilism 87
6. A Degenerative and Regenerative Economics of Philanthropy and Gift 92
7. Culture—for the Price of Admission 95
8. Toward a Topography of Financial Transactions 97
9. Faith, Hope, and Love: Elements of an Appreciative Economy 103

PART III
A WEALTH OF TRANSFORMATION:
INTERVIEWS EXPLORING MONEY AND SPIRIT

An Interview with Jacob Needleman 113
An Interview with an Anonymous Donor 121
An Interview with Charles Terry 129
An Interview with Krystyna Jurzykowski 138
An Interview with Paul Mackay 146
An Interview with Michael Spence 155
An Interview with Lynne Twist 164
An Interview with Betsy Taylor 172
An Interview with Wangari Maathai 183

EPILOGUE: Money Weighs and Means 193

Introduction

Money Being Transformed

MONEY IS A MARVELOUS WORK of mind, legal tender, and economic convenience. It was invented for the sake of efficiency, used by agreement, and circulated as a storehouse of value for goods and services. Money is thus singularly complex. As it moves about the globe, changing its face and flowing from hand to hand, it carries intentionality, fosters social contracts through transactions, and accounts for an otherwise invisible world of values.

This is a great weight to bear, or rather, a weight we bring to bear on our financial life. The journey inward to understand money in the deepest sense and to become more conscious participants in financial transactions with the world leads us to grapple with the "money-self" while working to meet the material needs of others so that our economic needs are met through their work. This formulation describes a threefold virtuous cycle—one that represents a radical transformation from our current world circumstance, which tends to revolve around and end with self-interest, unsupportable accumulation, and fear born of never-enough.

The concept of self-interest in economic life was never questioned as a valid or sound operating principle at any point during my education. It did not really dawn on me how problematic and illusionary it is, until I began my inquiry into money, spirit, and human behavior. I have worked in an advisory capacity with many individuals and groups who are passionate about the work they do and who care deeply about what they are accomplishing for the benefit of the world. However, when it came time to address questions about money, salaries, and fees, those same people would enjoin the conversation as if they were a different set of personalities. Something, some inexplicable energy, presented itself as a shadow—passion turned to rancor and distrust, care turned to anxiety. This strange disconnection between what I would call public cultural selves and private economic selves has been acknowledged by most of those organizations. Taken together they constitute a problematic pattern. It should come as no surprise that virtually all of these same organizations were short of financial and human resources and were having trouble attracting the funds they needed, especially through gifts.

The disconnection between public and private selves, particularly around money, became the center of my inquiry, beginning first with myself. I quickly realized that the inquiry was endless, that it would require a continual reflective process. My hope and purpose is for this inquiry to serve as an invitation to others to engage in their own, both as individuals and as organizations striving to transform the world through transforming themselves first. This is not practice what you preach, but rather practice what you hope the future may look like. It is in the spirit of encouraging and informing a real and needed process, a reimagining of money, that this collection of writing is offered.

The structure of this book is founded upon three stages of a virtuous cycle from inner-private to outer-public reflection and action. The first part, "The Poetics of Money," is an exploration of money as a cultural and spiritual phenomenon. Some of the Western world's story of money has been told through the eyes and hands of artists since medieval times, much of it in the context of religious- and morality-based art. However, since money has become a matter of noetics, a science of consciousness, rather than an article of faith or belief, contemplation of money's role in contemporary life is to be found in journals of psychology and on business pages, even as we struggle with its sudden disappearance and reappearance through the economic roller coaster, the bubbles and debacles of our time.

Because money is so deeply connected—I would even say identified—with our psyche and identity, it is a natural mystery, one tied to our perceptions, and more important, to our capacity for real self-knowledge. There are those who hold that money is entirely neutral; it is nothing more than what we make of it. It is a physical object—paper, metal, or plastic—with no innate meaning except in its use. Such a view leaves us to wrestle with our emotions as projections onto the object of money. A more subjective view says that money is energy. This perspective puts us in the position of money being a direct extension and bearer of our energetic or spiritual selves, that which inspires and motivates us to breathe and engage with life. Thus, its meaning is inseparable from whatever meaning we author for ourselves. The challenge here is to find enough detachment from the transactional experience to be sure it is accountable in an objective way. There is much to be said about both perspectives, and both are necessary and inseparable. Thus, "The Poetics of Money" explores money as inner experience and as cultural or behavioral phenomenon—inside looking out, outside looking in.

The second part, "A Topography of Transactions," is an attempt to take an experience-based approach to financial transactions—to their different qualities and how we might understand our internal sentient map as we navigate the economic world—and gauge our responses to them. My working assumption is that, just as the three primary colors serve as the irreducible fundamentals of all color theory and practice, money has three forms that serve as primaries for all manner of financial transactions carried out in economic life. This innovative perspective was first posited by Rudolf Steiner in his lectures on Economics given in 1922. (See *New Principles in Economics*, SteinerBooks 2010). Steiner viewed money as having three basic transactional forms: purchase, loan, and gift.

Upon this platform, I have attempted to develop a more elaborated and practical theory of transactions as they occur in space and across time. For example, transparency is essential for the purpose of accounting, which is an outer manifestation, as well as for establishing trust, an inner condition. The way we use money requires that we view our relationship to it and to our partners-in-transaction in a manner appropriate to the essential and particular nature of the transactions and their purposes. The matrix I developed is nothing more than a guide to exploring an individual's money-self, in order to understand what motivates and transpires through financial transactions from material needs to destiny paths.

Part three, "A Wealth of Transformation," is devoted to exploring the voices of those who have taken on transforming themselves and the world through rethinking the use of money, economic practices, and social finance.

The interviews explore personal journeys of coming to terms with social injustice; philanthropy based on intuition; investing with a vision of future value; and simply good common sense in relation to our limited natural resources and the aspects of life, such as caring and learning, that are dearly valued but excluded from economic theory. Through the work of these individuals who have developed new perspectives on how to live their values—in some cases, despite difficult personal consequences—we gain insight into the strategies of the philanthropic mind, system change, and social transformation. It has been my privilege to serve and witness these voices over the last eight years. They are time-bound, timely, and they are timeless. Through their accomplishments, clarity, and capacity for reflection, the interviewees have been my teachers and have conveyed here a true wealth of transformation.

I would be remiss if I did not mention one other source of inspiration for my inquiry, though there is no essay about or interview with them in the book. When I entered the money-space, I was hard put to find historical precedents for the inquiry, though there are other contemporaries wrestling brilliantly with related questions. It was not until I was introduced by a friend to the work of the Knights Templar that I could find the spiritual stream in which to locate myself. The Templars, known in current culture primarily through references in films and historical novels, were active primarily from the early twelfth to the early fourteenth centuries. The basic history, their bravery as fighters in the crusades, is well known. They were a religious order, authorized by the pope, and reported solely to him. Thus, they were free from the operating hierarchy and politics of the church establishment. What most drew my attention is that at their beginning—they were a small group of only nine—they requested and received permission to establish their offices in a palace built on the ruins of the ancient Temple of Solomon in Jerusalem. Their first work was an intensive study of the mystery of the Temple's architecture in order to rebuild it. This was deeply spiritual research, as it embodied ancient esoteric wisdom, and little is known about it, though there are many theories. As one of the conditions for occupying the temple site, they pledged to protect from thieves those making religious pilgrimages along the road from the port of Jaffa to Jerusalem. This task was their exoteric or public work. They developed a system for protecting the pilgrims' valuable gold by issuing credit notes for the gold that could be redeemed for equal value at any of a number of Templar's offices along the way or in Jerusalem. Thus, a prototype "banking" system for the West was formed that was based upon trust, a banking system that had a basis in esoteric knowledge and philosophy, and also an exoteric purpose that accompanied others on their quests. As trustees of the wealth of others, the Templars never claimed anything for themselves personally, but rather their own needs were met through the offices of the order. Because of this trust, the order received many gifts, which enabled them to finance the building of chapels throughout Europe and the Holy lands and to establish a thriving system of trades and businesses. Much has been made of their demise as an order. In short, by the dawn of the fourteenth century, the Templar order had grown exponentially, and Philip the Fair, the king of France, was jealous of their power and desirous of their wealth. On October 13, 1307, he arrested Templars throughout France and falsely branded them as heretics. The order was dissolved by an Apostolic decree in 1312. Their history is, of course, far more complicated than my telling of it. But, what they stood for and acted on behalf of has deep personal resonance for me; I am convinced that their foreshortened mission somehow holds significance for our time.

We are now a secular society in the West, beyond the age of religious orders as they were then needed, in which money has become disconnected from our spirituality as it has more and more served the forces of materialism—greed and power. The Templars understood the virtue and constructive value of integration between their inner and outer lives. They connected inner devotional practice and related outer activity of service to others through finance and protective accompaniment. I stand in the spirit of this historical stream with the intention of reimagining money for a healthier future, and, from that place, offer the words that comprise this collection of thoughts, experiences, and, I trust, wisdom.

John Bloom

PART I

The Poetics of Money

THE TRIBUTE MONEY, Masaccio (1401–1428)

1. Tribute Paid

At the Intersection of Spirit and Money

The realms of spirit and religion, engaged as they are with the non-material world, nevertheless must find a way to work in a world that trades in money. That religious organizations can be tax-exempt in the United States is proof enough of that. And in Germany, for example, tax dollars actually flow through the government to support the churches. While this is definitely not an essay on the separation of church and state, it is about the intersection of religious or spiritual practice, a private matter, and the world of money, which tends to be a public matter. Societies treat these matters in ways that reflect their belief systems and political agreements, and there are many variants. While one could make a life study of this topic, my hope is that two perspectives, conveyed in two paintings and a poem, will shed a little light on those differences as stimulus for considering our own inherited or consciously developed assumptions, beliefs, and agreements.

In an episode from the New Testament, the Gospel of Matthew 17:24, Peter is confronted by a tax collector. Peter promises the collector that the tax will be paid; but, when he reports this to Jesus, Jesus establishes through logical inquiry that they have no real obligation to pay the tax. However, in order "not to give offense to them," Jesus instructs Peter to catch a fish in whose mouth he would find a coin to pay the tax.

This scene was famously rendered by Masaccio as one of his many frescos in the Brancacci Chapel of Santa Maria della Carmine in Florence, 1426-1428. In *Tribute Money*, Peter is on the left side of the painting taking the coin from the fish's mouth and then, in a kind of time-sweep panorama, paying the tax on the right side. The aesthetic magic of this filmic representation serves as a delicate reminder of the quiet miracle in the biblical sequence. That the coin was found in the mouth of a fish is laden with Christian symbolism. Jesus well understood the revolutionary nature of the new religious impulse he was bringing to humanity, birthed as it was out of Judaism and in the context of the, not yet Holy, Roman Empire. At that time Christianity was nascent, and Jesus' response was conciliatory. He knew that he had enemies and detractors in both camps, and was careful to distinguish political treachery from more innocent spiritually-motivated behavior. In this frame of reference, money and taxes are the stuff of politics.

The politics of taxes comes up again later in Matthew in 22:17-22. But this time, the outcome is quite different. When Jesus is approached by another tax collector, he responds to the disingenuous question of whether it is lawful to pay taxes to Caesar by first asking to see the money piece required for the tax. He then asks whose likeness and inscription is on the coin. The tax collector answers that it is Caesar's. After castigating the collector for being a hypocrite, Jesus then speaks his oft quoted line: "Render therefore to Caesar the things that are Caesar's, and to God the things that are God's." Jesus could identify the hypocrisy because he knew that the collector's own religious practice would not really have him subject to Caesar's tax, but that the collector and his fellow Pharisees and Herodites had in some ways already sold out to Rome. Jesus also knew that the question was part of a scheme to frame him as an enemy of the state. And so, the collectors, caught off guard by the veracity of his statements, were forced to abandon their attempt to entrap Jesus. In this case, Jesus was pointing to the distinction between matters of state and spirit, and that each has different terms of engagement.

In *The Tribute Money* (1518), in the Dresden Gallery in Germany, Titian renders the moment of the transactional conversation from Matthew 22:17 in

THE TRIBUTE MONEY: CHRIST AND THE PHARISEE
Titian (c. 1488–1576)

a highly editorial manner. The Herodian character is painted in a dark, murky palette, and the distribution of light does not follow pictorial logic. Jesus seems to emanate his own light. Also, Jesus is not actually touching the money, "filthy lucre" as it became. What strikes me as essential, however, is that Jesus is looking into the other man's eyes and thus establishes an energetic dynamic quite separate from the hand-to-hand transaction below. This kind of intense eye contact is not a common part of financial transactions, as far as I remember or practice.

It speaks to a quality of engagement that directly touches the other party (for better or worse) and, in doing so, validates the level of relationship necessary to bringing a new consciousness to money. As Titian portrayed it, Jesus' gaze is disarming and serves to unmask the deceit of the other—the power of spirit over the power of money, the rule of moral law over the laws of the state.

This moral force takes on a different tone in the poem "Deciding" by William Stafford, who wrote from a modern, and less doctrinal, vantage point. Further, he was awake to a nuance of an American consciousness that moves beyond the duality of heaven and earth, spirit and matter, even good and evil, as played out in the scenes from the Gospel of Matthew. Here is Stafford's poem:

> One mine the Indians worked had
> gold so good they left it there
> for God to keep.
>
> At night sometimes you think
> your way that far, that deep,
> or almost.
>
> You hold all things or not, depending
> not on greed but whether they suit what
> life begins to mean.
>
> Like those workers you study what moves,
> what stays. You bow, and then, like them,
> you know—
>
> What's God, what's world, what's gold.

To make the comparison between money and gold requires an imaginative leap; but in the context of the poem, gold is a kind of currency. Gold clearly has value as a precious metal, with a long history of representing the deep curse of materialism. In the myth of King Midas, for example, everything he touches turns to gold, including his daughter. Gold also has a long history of representing consciousness, as the alchemical transformation from the base metal lead. Stafford takes us past this duality of the spiritual (God) and the material (world) into a kind of triptychal configuration in which gold actually embodies the potential for both in its physicality and aura. It is the genius of this poem that expresses the inner capacity of the miners to know how to transcend the simple duality, and instead to be in both places at once—and thus in the third place. Jesus was an exemplar and teacher of this conscious capacity to see both what belongs to the world and what belongs in the realm of spirit, and beyond that to be able to discern and point out when the two fall out of integrity. This kind of knowing is intuitional, and worthy of being emulated, even if one is likely to fail.

Money calls upon our lower or desire nature—what Stafford points to as greed—because it is associated with the realms of rights and power, and is synonymous with access to material goods and services. Through government-issued currency, the state regulates the financial transactional sector to a degree, especially interest rates, and thus also gains domination over taxation. Taxation is a material part of a citizen's participation in the commonwealth, our required share of the cost of government. Further, because we are so dependent upon money and the marketplace to provide for us in our evolved citified culture, money carries with it dominion over our sense of well-being, our sense of self-sufficiency—a place dangerously close to our identity and spirit-self.

However, it is not surprising to find a sense of well-being and abundance present in some of the so-called poorest communities, where, provided that the sense of community itself is intact, a gift economy is the true currency and taxes are irrelevant. This somewhat idyllic picture points to the presence of spirit in the care people have and practice for each other. The eye-to-eye gaze depicted by Titian is one level of *communitas* or communion that Jesus was already practicing with his disciples. How money changes hands is another level—one often less attended to because of money's long materialistic history and perpetuated by our own inherited assumptions about it. Like the alchemists and the Indian miners, we have an opportunity to transform money by not being ruled by our desire nature, but rather by seeing that money is connected to our intentions whether moral-ethical or disingenuous. Money is both material and spiritual. Our task is to find that third place where both realities are always present and potent, and also remain integrated.

DANAE AND THE SHOWER OF GOLD
Titian (c. 1488–1576)

2. Coining a Myth

Titian : *Danae and the Shower of Gold*

Myths are meant to be told and retold. The archetypes they contain are deep human patterns of character, action, and circumstance that maintain their essences despite manifold variations. The literal and figurative coexist with great comfort and have meanings that both transcend time and are simultaneously embedded in a particular time and place. The language, the images, and the choices in any teller's presentation are conditioned by prevailing cultural norms along with her or his personal history. With each retelling, a myth is given new life.

The artists of the Italian Renaissance had the joy of rediscovering the art of ancient Greece and Rome, much of which had been physically buried for centuries. The excavations sparked the merging of a scientific and anthropocentric view of the world, as epitomized in the development of perspective drawing and a fascination with the fluid harmony of forms and proportions typified by classic Greek sculptures. In some sense, the duality of spirit and matter became a central issue. In choosing to paint the mythological story of Danae and the shower of gold, Titian, a Venetian master in the High Renaissance, addressed this duality in a very direct way.

In short, the Greek myth goes like this: Danae was a princess of Argos in the Greek Peloponnesos, the only child of King Acrisius and Eurydice. When Acrisius goes to visit the Oracle at Delphi hoping to find out if he will ever have a son, instead, he is told that he will be killed by his future grandson. To prevent this, Acrisius has Danae and her servant locked up in a subterranean chamber. However, the story of Danae's confinement reaches Zeus on Mount

Olympus. When Zeus goes to investigate, he immediately falls in love with the beautiful Danae. Zeus then impregnates Danae in the guise of a golden shower, and from this union, she bears a son, Perseus. When her father learns what has happened, he places Danae and her infant son in a wooden chest and sets it adrift on the sea. Thanks to the help of Zeus's brother, Neptune, the god of the sea, the chest drifts ashore on the island of Seriphas, where Dictys, a fisherman, discovers them and welcomes them into his home. Perseus grows up to become the first of the great legendary heroes of Greek mythology, rescuing Androm-eda from a sea monster and slaying the terrible Medusa.

The scene of Zeus as the golden shower that Titian has chosen to depict from this story shows the shower of gold as coins falling in two directions, one following the path of light in which Danae is bathed, the other dropping into the upheld apron of the servant. The shower of gold is a metaphysical or alchemical concept in itself, and so, representing a quality of light that could carry the otherworldly power of procreation, yet have some recogniz-able (material form), was quite a dilemma.

Titian solved this dilemma by setting up a contrast in his approach to rendering the coins and also between the tonal and energetic qualities of the two figures. The coins falling toward Danae have a light, ethereal quality; they fall like feathers. Danae lies bathed in light, vulnerable, unprotected. In contrast, the coins directed toward the servant's apron move more like projec-tiles, traveling with force and focus. They emerge from dark, ominous clouds, casting their shadows across the servant on the right side of the painting. The servant figure moves aggressively to gather the coins, with a sweeping gesture of greed.

The purpose of my close analysis of this painting is to highlight the fact that Titian could understand and render golden "coins" as still linked to the ancient and archetypal past of spiritual power—here the coins are a formal expression of that power. On one hand, he equates light, gold, and creative consciousness, while on the other, he acknowledges the more overshadowed, modern reality of wealth, gold, and greed.

Imprisoned together in the cave, the two characters react as polar opposites to the sudden abundance of wealth. It is easy to fall into judgment about the two; but they are both archetypal characters, and, as such, reflections of both reside in all of us. For example, in the face of abundance I know I have a self-less part of me that wants to transform it and distribute it for the good. I also know the part of me that wants to gather it up and hold on to it because "there is never enough."

Thus is the power of art: to tell a mythological story on a grand scale that also has all the feeling of being the important news of the day.

BARRELS OF MONEY

Victor Dubreuil (1880–1910)

3. Trumped Money

Value and the Eye of the Beholder

Given the precision with which Victor Dubreuil selected his subject matter and applied his *trompe l'oeil* technique to this still life, one can assume a certain degree of social commentary. Some historical context is important in order to understand his inferences. The 1890s was the age of the "robber barons"; the accumulation of wealth by the few had an impoverishing consequence for the rest of the population in the United States. From the populist standpoint, there was great mistrust of the reigning powers—bankers and government. And there was good reason. Those in charge of monetary policy were wrestling with the gold-backed currency while at the same time re-issuing "greenbacks" that were in fact pure fiat money—that is to say money issued on faith with no real or agreed upon objective valuation basis. Greenbacks were first issued to help pay for Civil War expenses and were blessed as legal tender. As with our current money, it was a completely self-referential currency in that you could go to the Federal Reserve or the issuer and you were assured only one thing, you would receive another bill of the same denomination or an equivalent total of one you were exchanging. Of course, fiat money can be issued without limits because it is not pegged to any other measure. In other words, one could have barrels of it, though its actual purchase value would depend upon who actually trusted that it had any value in the first place. Given Dubreuil's capacity for visual replication, I imagine he enjoyed the trope of counterfeit as a commentary on what was real in the first place.

The issuance and supply of currency have always been suspended between the poles of quantity and quality. Consumers tend to desire quantity since this gives them more purchase power, at least until the currency devaluates, while producers prefer the qualitative because this supports rising value until it brings about a cost of production and prices too high to afford. And, of course, the debate between gold-backed currency and fiat currency is something of a reflection of this polarity, but in a complicated context of politics, power, and class consciousness. Our present-day financial system meets the consumer's wish for quantity not so much through the issuance of fiat currency as by deregulating a banking system that provides unrestrained credit or indebtedness (mostly at predatory rates, unfortunately).

Dubreuil's choice to portray the money in barrels is a populist reference. Barrels were common storage for everything from wine to hardware; but to find them in an isolated space where the only identifier is a stone floor constructed in harlequin-like sections is a deliberate contradiction—another visual joke one might assume. And, of course, he plays with the size and scale of the bills in relation to the barrels, an accepted standard of measure. Through his representational style, Dubreuil has much to say about money and our assumptions about it. His work is somewhat of a morality play stage set that teases us into accepting the factotum simply through its means of representation—that is until its credibility comes into question under analysis. While *Barrels of Money* is full of wit and irony, the irony is doubled by the fact that this was one of the first works of art collected by the Federal Reserve Bank, where it now resides in the vault-like confines of the central bank of the United States.

4. The Other Invisible Hand

Money and Its Subtle Influence on Social Life

I recently came across an intriguing article in *The New York Times*, "Just Thinking About Money Can Turn the Mind Stingy," by Benedict Carey.[1] The author was trying to place the seemingly surprising findings of a recent research report into a historical, human-behavioral context. This *New York Times* article was based on a research report published in *Science* entitled "The Psychological Consequences of Money." The researchers found that their test subjects acted in either a more or less community-minded manner depending on whether they had been exposed to neutral or money-based background content in the task materials they were given. Further, these behavior patterns were evident regardless of race, class, gender, age, or any other group. It is a fascinating study, one which confirms what I [and probably many others] have experienced over many years of working with issues of money in organizations. That is: When money or financial issues are at play in the context of decision making, even the most socially conscious, warm-hearted people tend to act in an anti-social manner.

The following is the abstract for the research published in the *Science* article:

Money has been said to change people's motivation (mainly for the better) and their behavior toward others (mainly for the worse). The results of nine experiments suggest that money brings about a self-sufficient

---

1. *New York Times*: Science Times Section, November 21, 2006.

orientation in which people prefer to be free of dependency and dependents. Reminders of money, relative to non-money reminders, led to reduced requests for help and reduced helpfulness toward others. Relative to participants primed with neutral concepts, participants primed with money preferred to play alone, work alone, and put more physical distance between themselves and a new acquaintance.[2]

In short, when money is introduced into the mix, the default reaction is to withdraw into a self-centered or egocentric posture and away from a more altruistic view that includes concern for others and recognition of our real dependence upon one another. Neither the *New York Times* nor the *Science* articles addressed whether this is bred-in-the-bone or learned behavior. This is a challenging question because money and the financial systems of which it is a part are relatively late entries into the evolutionary stream of human consciousness. It is a likely bet that money first emerged as a technology of transactional agreement in the service of furthering human economy. Only more recently has the acquisition of it become an end unto itself and a legitimate measure of worth. Though I could not make a direct correlation between this latter shift and the behavior demonstrated by the experiment, my sense is that money is now so deeply connected to our sense of identity or being and our sense of safety that any inflection upon those senses will instantaneously and unconsciously adversely affect our social or relational capacities. It is a challenging place to be so bound to something we can neither really own (we have only a right of use) nor control the value of.

The authors of the research study have tapped into one of the great mysteries and, probably, ironies of our time. Namely: Self-reliance is an important spiritual ideal from the point of view of individual freedom, but a misleading illusion from the point of view of interdependence in our economic life. What they found, I think, is that with the background money mind-set, the subjects no longer operated as socially normal, as defined by the neutral mind-set group.

---

2. *Science*: "The Psychological Consequences of Money"; Kathleen D. Vohs, Nicole L. Mead, and Miranda R. Goode; Nov. 17, 2006: Vol. 314. no. 5802, pp. 1154–1156.

The money-minded separated themselves either out of fearfulness and protection or because they felt that they did not need the others. In either case, by placing themselves apart they were denying consciously or unconsciously the social significance of, and their real dependence on, an economic system that somehow punishes or benefits them. The outcome of the research points to a level of disintegration between inner and outer life that has had increasingly powerful social implications for everyone, and is probably one (of many) of the driving forces of the wealth gap that has expanded so drastically in recent years. The more one "separates" oneself from the social body, the more one has to accumulate resources to meet one's own needs. And accumulation is the name of the game; a mistaken substitution of net worth for self worth.

For the *New York Times* article, Carey interviewed George Loewenstein, professor of economics and psychology, Carnegie Mellon University, Pittsburgh. Loewenstein responded to the findings of the research: "We know there is a civilizing side to money, that people acting in a self-interested fashion depend on fellow human beings in a community and tend to treat them fairly.... But this study shows its pernicious side, how the pursuit of money can be isolating." This response identifies even more layers of complexity. It is fair to point to the civilizing side of money since it does make transacting efficient in our economic life, as each transaction is also an embedded agreement about value exchange or cost and use of funds. It is also fair to point to our dependence upon our fellow human beings as a reason to treat them equitably—a version of the golden rule. But what the study shows is that, in our current culture, money and self-interest are so inextricable that fairness has become a matter of priority rather than a bedrock value—especially if you are on the wealth side of the gap.

As individuals, each of us will have a response to the implications of this important research and the ensuing dialogue, if we care to. On a personal level, I look at my work as serving or meeting the needs of others. And I appreciate that others have made the clothes and grown the food that I and my family purchase as consumers. To me this is the oversimplified essence of economics; it is a picture of interdependence. From a certain perspective, one could remove all the money and financial transactions and still have a functioning economy. By this I mean we could still work to find the resources (food, shelter, clothing) to meet each other's needs with human resources, motivated by a sense of responsibility and community. But money is ever-present and powerful, and we need to realize on personal, community, and policy levels the injustice that has emerged from an economy that is essentially ego-centric. That we can barely do anything without having money these days indicates that money is almost always coloring our social and economic experience. Thus, the findings of the researchers about money's subtle influence on behavior have significant implications for cultural, political, and economic life in general. The findings indicate the inner and personal work we must do in order to effect social transformation—if that is our wish.

When Adam Smith named the original metaphor of "the invisible hand" in *The Wealth of Nations*, he was making an oblique religious reference to a higher being at work in the economy. What the new research identifies through scientific methodology is the other invisible hand, our unconscious self at work in our economic behavior. The transformative work, then, is to become conscious of the unconscious influence money has on each of us—to bring it out of the shadows—and then to align and integrate our financial practices with our deepest values.

5. Reforging Adam Smith

Beyond the Gates of Self-Interest

It seems that the shadow of Adam Smith's principle of benevolently motivated self-interest, which he so eloquently articulated, now looms over our adumbrated economy. Part of that principle indicates that if we are true to our natural instincts, we will recognize that our own self-interest is served through our interest in the well-being of others. On the positive side, one can see the origins of modern philanthropy in this construct. But, what is one to make of self-interest as it applies to the Federal Reserve Bank bailout (granted through guarantees) of a major investment house whose fortunes were tied to the subprime loan market? From Adam Smith, one might think that lenders would have an interest in the success of their borrowers. And perhaps some of the loan originators did have such an interest. But that disappeared as the loans were bundled, securitized, and sold; and the extractive investors fed their needs in total disconnection from the original purpose and relationship between the lenders and the borrowers. This looks more like a form of self-interest in which the predator simply harbors a natural interest in the survivability of its prey.

The shadow side of Smith's socio-economic theory is created when an individual's (or corporation's) self-interest turns to greed and suffers from the condition of "never-enoughness." In this light, it is important to note the strange-but-true rights of a corporation as equal to those of an individual. Both can celebrate the same freedoms and suffer the same diseases, and then be cured according to their wealth, class status, and access to power. What to make of the bitter difference between the speed with which the Federal Reserve and JP Morgan responded to the financial crisis of one of their own (creditors) versus the glacial and heavily politicized response to the conditions of the debtors? This is the worst case of self-interest, one of excluding "the other" for the benefit of the few—a kind of economic wealth-class protectionism. Likely, this is not the benevolent self-interest that Adam Smith had in mind. While this critique is not the primary focus of this article, it is its essential backdrop; and, it would be hard to ignore the irony when a captain of industry, such as Bill Gates, plays the Adam Smith card.

A friend recently sent me a transcript of the Economic Forum Speech that Bill Gates gave in Davos last year. It is remarkable for several reasons, not the least of which is that Gates was looking at Adam Smith's self-interest principle in a light that addresses and frames "the other" in terms of stark, real economic need (in which he includes computer technology) rather than a more generalized interest in fellow human beings. Gates also suggests that capitalism can find a way to solve the poverty it has been a part of creating; at the same time, his analysis of wealth creation and its concentration is direct and pointed. His is, of course, a privileged view, and he was speaking to a privileged audience. However, despite his inability to leave the market-driven, self-interested model and language behind, he was bringing renewed focus to what is essentially an altruistic concept—an awareness of interdependence and the limitations of a free-market economy devoid of any ethic other than profit and shareholder value.

The following are excerpts from his speech:

I believed that breakthroughs in technology could solve the key problems...but breakthroughs change lives only where people can afford to buy them—only where there is economic demand. And economic demand is not the same as economic need. There are billions of people who need the great inventions of the computer age, and many more basic needs as well. But they have no way of expressing their needs in ways that matter to markets. So they go without.

If we are going to have a serious chance of changing their lives, we will need another level of innovation. Not just technology innovation—we need system innovation.

Why do people benefit in inverse proportion to their need? Market incentives make that happen.... We have to find a way to make the aspects of capitalism that serve wealthier people serve poorer people as well.

The genius of capitalism lies in its ability to make self-interest serve the wider interest.... This system driven by self-interest is responsible for the great innovations that have improved the lives of billions. But to harness this power so it benefits everyone—we need to refine the system.

As I see it, there are two great forces of human nature: self-interest and caring for others. Capitalism harnesses self-interest in helpful and sustainable ways, but only on behalf of those who can pay.

Such a system would have a twin mission: making profits and also improving lives for those who don't fully benefit from market forces. To make the system sustainable, we need to use profit incentives whenever we can. At the same time, profits are not always possible when business tries to serve the very poor. In such cases, there needs to be another market-based incentive—and that incentive is recognition. Recognition enhances a company's reputation and appeals to customers; above all, it attracts good people to the organization.... The challenge is to design a system where market incentives, including profit and recognition, drive the change.

I like to call this new system creative capitalism.... This hybrid engine of self-interest and concern for others serves a much wider circle of people than can be reached by self-interest or caring alone.

System refinement and system innovation are always afoot in the capitalist-entrepreneurial mind set. But neither questions the basic assumptions of the system itself. I am not critiquing capitalism, but rather the interpretation of it that said at one time that laissez-faire and now free-markets is the only reasonable approach. This makes perfect sense if the people setting the rules are the ones most likely to benefit.

The abuses of the market and capital systems lie primarily in two arenas. The first and most obvious one is the economic sphere, where the underlying purpose is meeting people's material needs through the production of goods and services. In this arena, overproduction and overconsumption are the culprits, motivated just as Gates indicated by market share and profit. The consequences of this are starkly visible in the wealth gap. The second and less blatant arena is the domain of rights. Contrary to the basic principle of equality in the rights realm, those who have benefited most in the economic sector also have an interest in influencing government, law, policy, and financial markets in self-serving ways; for example, the credit card industry or its hired representatives, who craft and marshal through Congress the new bankruptcy law.

This is just one of many such aberrations of the rights process. For another perspective, it is interesting to look at who stands for *free* trade on one hand, and for *fair* trade on the other. Both are based on capitalist market models, yet their social outcomes are radically different. To be successful, fair trade necessitates an interest in the other.

It is significant that Gates is putting caring for others on a par with self-interest, as the former has gotten short shrift in modern economic life, except in the domain of philanthropy. But, does it make sense to try to meet the caring aspects through capitalism, no matter how creative that might be? I do not think there is any economics text that places caring in an economic framework. While our lives depend on it, it cannot be manufactured and it is "priceless." And by the way, when last I cared to reflect on it, caring seems like an infinitely renewable resource.

The problem is that the conventional tools of capitalism are not designed to sustain these deeply human life-sources. Bill Gates is suggesting recognition as the motivational tool to getting markets to support the needy. I suggest that this would be self-limiting: The stockholders would only go so far with it; it would wear thin in time; and it would most likely be misused to gain market shares, which are, in the end, essential to the character and purpose of capital markets.

There are, indeed, new or emerging tools to meet the economic needs of those outside the market economy, but they are not refinements of capitalism. Instead, they come under the general heading of complementary currencies. They are complementary because they are not meant to replace federal- or government-issued currencies; they are called currencies because they are a means of exchange in an interdependent self-governed economy. There are already numerous forms of complementary currencies solving social problems in many places around the world. The stories are profound and empowering. ACCESS Foundation is a keeper of some of these stories, as well as a resource for the field of complementary currencies. One system, called TimeBanks, is entirely based on time rather than money (www.timebanks.org). Such currencies are generated by the communities that will use them, and since they are under community control there can always be a sufficient amount. There is no purpose or value in restricting the circulation. They could be used to offset the problem that market solutions are not the answer to every socio-economic problem, just as technology can never solve moral dilemmas.

Complementary currencies are rooted in ancient traditions of gift exchange and community life. They are now re-emerging in new forms that call upon the human faculties of trust and community-spirit—faculties that we do not get to practice very often in an economic context. And yes, they are entirely dependent upon the new computer-based technologies for recording, tracking, and portability. So, in this sense, Bill Gates is right, and to be appreciated. But, technology even at its best is a means, not an end. The blessing is that there are social entrepreneurs who are using technology as part of solving the deeper systemic human problems that economic science has found intractable. Organizations developing complementary currencies need more time, more support, and more buy-in, so to speak. Their genius is that they are based upon the most timeless and effective concept in economic life: matching unused resources with unmet needs. This is not about manufacturing 3000 choices of each commodity to please the consumer market; rather, this is about making efficient use of what rises up from an inexhaustible (so far) resource—caring.

Fortunately, Bill Gates did not mention Adam Smith's proverbial invisible hand. That would have attached market forces to a divine purpose, which even the grand designer might have found offensive. But to elevate and celebrate caring as an economic reality is a gift and an opportunity for a whole new dialogue, one that looks beyond "creative capitalism" to a more decentralized and localized economic interdependence and pluralistic means of exchange. Capitalism is not "wrong," just limited. We need more and different meta-capital tools to incorporate the real need for and economic value of the intangibles that support, rather than suppress, the human spirit and its cultural expressions.

THE MONEY LENDER AND HIS WIFE

Quentin Metsys (c. 1466–1530)

6. An Inventory of Polarities

Quentin Metsys : *The Money Lender and His Wife*

This detail-rich painting, once owned by the famous painter Peter Paul Rubens and now owned by the Louvre Museum, lends itself easily to formal, semiotic, and historiographic analysis. This was likely a commissioned portrait, and its composition is structured with a classical symmetry. It was very much of its time in demonstrating aspects of daily life, and is full of moral messages and symbolic, particularly Christian, references. Metsys worked with such painstaking precision that the painting serves as a detailed visual inventory or accounting of the scene. However, because of this extreme order and precision the painting takes on a veneer of surrealism—in this case fact-is-stranger-than-fiction, as the saying goes. If you spend enough time with the image, what emerges is a complex of polarities, both evident and implied.

One simple example of this complexity is found in the reflection of a window on the curved surface of the oval mirror at the bottom of the painting. The perfectly rational explanation for the presence of the reflection of the window is that it serves as the source of the painting's illumination. The device is used by the artist to insert himself in the picture. But, when you look closely you will see that the window frame itself is also certainly meant as a reference to the crucifix.

The positive-negative (the "both-and") of this small element in the painting surfaces on a grander scale and is of more crucial significance in the powerful dynamic that plays out between the sacred and profane, between the religious script and the objects of material desire, a complementarity reinforced by the color schema. While the woman casually leafs through the illuminated manuscript open to a portrayal of the Madonna and Child, her attention is clearly drawn in the direction of the object the man is holding. This is the essential historical moment and message. To the knowledgeable person residing in Antwerp at the time—then a major center of mercantilism—every coin or other acceptable means of exchange had a story to tell about its issuer, provenance, and value system.

For the money lender, equivalency and value were a matter of judgment and negotiation. His living depended on these capacities. Devotion, on the other hand, was guided solely by the authority and dominion of the church. It is no small irony that in our current times, this situation has completely reversed. There are many, many religions and sects embracing a diversity of values and practices, but currencies are issued and governed by central, civil authorities. (No wonder that investment bankers are sometimes referred to as the new high priesthood, the bearers of mystical wisdom!)

Clearly this money lender did very well, well enough to have a portrait painted and to have bought the hand-illuminated religious book his wife is perusing. While Gutenberg had developed moveable type sixty-three years before this painting was made, it was not yet possible to replicate color images in books on the order seen in this painting. So, why is it that *she* holds the precious religious artifact, while *he* holds the precious metals and gems? Is there a gender polarity here as well? The answer is—of course. It is the same gender story line that has led to modern banks as the central issuing authorities for money, the agreements about its use, and the right to set lending rates to control the markets. And the same story line that in Western cultures withheld credit and financial standing to women until very recent times. Although that shift has changed the economic landscape, including the players and how decisions are made, the rules still have not really changed.

So, did Quentin Metsys paint the woman being drawn away from her devotional to admire the coins as a paean to the man, his profession, and his adoring wife, or was the artist a harbinger of a new impulse in the modern world, which was just emerging in the Renaissance? Namely, the notion that desire for wealth and the material world was overshadowing the desire for devotion and the holy. Metsys probably meant the painting as a cautionary tale, a moral teaching to warn of the dangers of such material distractions. The Bible says that it is easier for a camel to pass through the eye of a needle than for a rich man to get into heaven, after all. But that was back then.

Perhaps the most curious detail in the painting is the scene painted behind the couple, apparently out of the open door of the residence. Where the mirror in the forefront reflects the space in front of the plane of the painting, the scene outside the door takes us into what art historians call deep space. What we see there is an interchange between a youth and an old man. While those portrayed are enclosed in their interior space, one of tight definition and order, we see that in the exterior world wisdom and acculturation are continuing to cross generations through the convention of speech and the traditions of social interaction. Metsys has set up yet another polarity, and one quite relevant, for example, to my own practices and integrity around the values that I tell myself I hold and the way that I navigate the world. An internal dialogue between my spirit-self and my money-self is ongoing, as in the interior space of the painting. Further, I strive to bring the intelligence gained there into integrity with my behavior in transacting with the world—which I find generally operating with diverse values and messages. This is no easy work, especially when I look at it on the level of the meticulous and excruciating detail that Quentin Metsys shows me. A work of art such as this is an invitation to reflection. What was real to the artist at the time has also tapped into an archetypal story—the polarity of spirit and matter—that transcends time.

BEGGARS AT THE DOOR
Rembrandt van Rijn (1606–1669)

7. Begging to Differ

Charity at the Threshold

Not long ago, a friend ceremoniously presented me with a begging bowl as a token of appreciation. That bowl now contains an origami-folded snail (slow money) and a rabbit (fast money) made from dollar bills. The constant presence of the bowl got me thinking about the practice of begging as a spiritual tradition and as I experience it on the streets of San Francisco.

As I walk or drive along, many people hold signs out asking for help, which invariably raises in me an unwelcome inner dilemma. Some of the signs seem tragic, some clever; most are scribbled on old cardboard, and much the worse for wear. The people displaying the signs are sad exemplars of the human condition, and their presence is compelling. My personal dilemma has many dimensions of elicited response—pity, guilt, anger at a system (of which I am a part) that makes for such a dehumanizing situation, as well as the uncomfortable reminder of my own privilege. I am enervated by my inability to reconcile such impoverished conditions with a place where there is so much wealth.

Begging has a rich history, storied as social commentary through literature and art, and treated as emblematic and instructive of one's responsibility to care for the other, the less fortunate. The dynamic of cross-class interaction and the assumptions, both true and false, that are played out in that dynamic are the stuff of drama. Begging and the charity it draws forth are part of a moral or religious cosmology of wholeness, and charitable acts have their own reward.

The seven-paneled altarpiece painted in 1504 by the Master of Alkmaar in the church of St. Lawrence, the Netherlands, portrays the seven works of charity through which one could secure a place in heaven: feeding the hungry

FEEDING THE HUNGRY

Master of Alkmaar (1490–1510)

(shown here), refreshing the thirsty, clothing the naked, burying the dead, receiving travelers, visiting the sick, and comforting prisoners. In this case, the beggar served the spiritual progress of the donor by providing an opportunity to exercise virtue. The beggar's condition did not symbolize injustice; it was nothing more than a fact of life, an object of pity. Thus, the work of art was not intended to serve as a polemic call for systemic change, which would have been outside the bounds of the mores of the time.

Another thread in the history of begging comes through the Buddhist stream of renunciation of worldly goods. Buddhist monks carry their begging bowls as part of their work in helping to bring about new spiritual consciousness in the world, as well as for their own initiation. This tradition has also found expression in the Christian "West." Inspired by the personal epiphanic experience of Francis of Assisi, his followers became mendicants as part of their evangelical work in the world, holding community property rather than private ownership as essential to furthering their sacrifice of self for the good of God. This is a far cry from begging in order to meet one's basic needs.

Such begging is one of the most unfortunate conditions to which a person can be reduced; yet, in a spiritual or religious context, it is practiced as a path to enlightenment. In the former, it does not seem to be a preferred choice; instead it is a social consequence. In the latter, the practice is taken as a totally conscious, self-imposed choice. Regardless of whether poverty is imposed by external circumstances or taken up voluntarily as a personal path, both require a committed trust in the world, and both are conditioned on vulnerability. Both extremes share the quality of a threshold experience that places the beggar at the edge of existence and the gift as a virtuous or spiritual deed and a bridge across that existential chasm.

In this line of thinking about begging, a dear friend told me about Cyber-beg.org and its kindred host of sites such as cyberbeggar.com, donate2me.com, and ePanhandle.com. Given all the emotions evoked by the interaction between beggar and donor, this new virtual process is intriguing in the anonymity and safety it makes possible for the beggar, complemented by a capacity for reach that goes well beyond a stream of passersby. To set up a begging site, I imagine one first has to self-identify as a beggar, putting aside all the stigma and cultural baggage, at least for the time being. This seems to me to be the fundamental shift of consciousness made possible by the aforementioned safety of the virtual space. [I admit here my concern about how presumptive this assertion may be, as I do not identify myself as a beggar.] I can certainly see the advantage to the beggar as a way to present his or her case without feeling judged by others, and without the physical strain of the act itself. The opportunity to tell one's story to whoever might listen or read definitely has value.

But, as a possible donor, why would I go out of my way to find such a site, where I know I will find active "begging," when I prefer to avoid such pleas in my daily travels? Am I wishing to have my heartstrings pulled? Given my own take on this, I wonder what kind of person might seek or take pleasure in reading about the tragedies of others—unless the search actually started as a desire to be charitable. That such sites exist is a sign of the times, revealing both the shadows and the opportunities.

Here is how Cyberbeg introduces itself (from the "about us" page of the website):

> Cyberbeg.com offers people hope. This site provides a way for financially unfortunate people to connect with those who may donate. Some may compare it to a lottery or the classifieds, but we like to think of it as a site dedicated to helping people. Before Cyberbeg.com, the financially unfortunate had no way of asking for help. Now, through Cyberbeg.com, requests are broadcasted for donators to view. The creators of Cyberbeg.com send the best of luck to all of those who need help and a sincere thanks to those who have donated to these worthy causes.

This represents a new kind of marketplace for begging—competitive, comparative, based primarily upon access to the web and then the quality of the written language. However, as I read the appeals I was inwardly experiencing the same unwanted dilemma of the interest-in, along with the wish-it-weren't-so, but now with a new addition—the rising sense of being a voyeur. In an attempt to understand this new mechanism and venue in the gift economy, I had chosen to enter its domain not to beg or donate—the site's primary reason for being—but rather to see what and how people represent their needs. Their stories are compelling, and I am sure they are mostly true, notwithstanding the necessary legal disclaimer; but in the end I felt more like a consumer than a donor, even though each of the entries has its own donate-now button. I do not know whether this feeling is conditioned by my accustomed use of the internet for information-seeking and shopping, or because my intuitive donor process is not activated by the virtual nature of the venue. I do know that charity is literally and figuratively a gesture of the heart and of love. Despite all the begging in the world, stepping into that gesture is also a threshold experience of my own making and one that I take in a measured way.

As I am writing this essay on Martin Luther King's birthday, it seems entirely appropriate to close with his words:

> Pity may represent little more than the impersonal concern which prompts the mailing of a check, but true sympathy is the personal concern which demands the giving of one's soul.

It is possible to consider Cyberbeg as the new, virtual begging bowl. When one registers a need on the website, it is clearly out of an inner decision or commitment, sometimes desperate, to seek gifts by "wandering" through cyberspace. My wish is that by donating online, the donor also has a meaningful and hopeful experience.

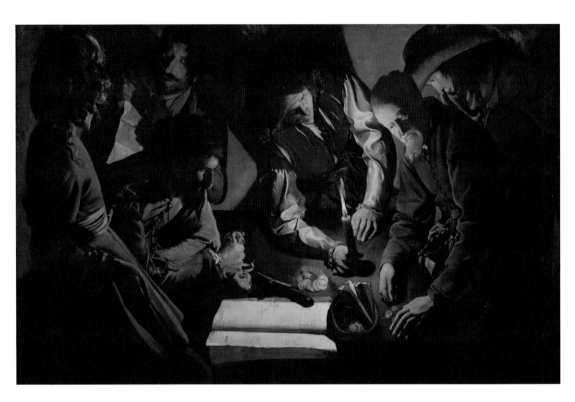

THE PAYMENT OF TAXES

Georges de la Tour (1593–1652)

8. Economic Chiaroscuro

Georges de La Tour : *The Payment of Taxes*

Georges de La Tour was a master of painting scenes illuminated by candle-light. It was his chief compositional and organizing principle and became his signature approach throughout his work. His portrayal and storytelling revolve around the single-point light source of a candle flame, its warm glow and sharp shadows. Although he used traditional perspective, with this technique the sense of a vanishing point is absent and there is no distant resting point for the eye; rather, the viewer is implicitly included and held in the radiant, taut space of the dramatic scene. This is visual theater; it is about directorial as well as painterly decisions.

The story portrayed in *The Payment of Taxes* is about an elderly man who has opened his purse to pay his taxes to the collector. There is an official registry or book of accounts open on the table. The collector himself stares intently at the collection of coins on the table and at the same time, as if unconsciously, tightly clutches a money bag. The figure in the center is leaning in toward the old man to hold the candle closer, presumably so that the old man can see better—though, of course, then they will all see the coins better. Judging by the expression on the old man's face, this is not a pleasant experience. His worried look seems not only about digging deeply into his purse to pay what is due, but also about his resignation to the fate of never having quite enough. The luxuriantly clad figure whose face is turned away from the viewer is either a military officer or some government official. Given de La Tour's interest in character and expression, the facelessness of the representative of the state is fully intentional. He is part of the group on the left side of the table who stand on the side of power. Hidden within a deep and encompassing shadow, they have been rendered less visible than the figures on the right hand side, where the light brings forth their individual humanity and elicits a note of sympathy from the viewer.

This particular painting marked the beginning of Georges de La Tour's so called "night paintings." Instead of the concept of night, I would frame an understanding of this painting (and his others in a similar mode) around the concept of interiority—the interior spaces that we inhabit both outwardly and physically, as well as inwardly and psychologically. On one hand, this seems somewhat obvious; on the other, this is not necessarily understood from the deeper perspective of how the interior and exterior are linked and integrated. Financial transactions, especially paying taxes, often highlight a lack of integration between inner and outer behavior.

There is apparently no definitive historical or literary interpretation of this painting.[1] De La Tour sometimes rendered biblical stories in the characters and staging of his own time, but there are not enough referents included in this painting to assign that kind of meaning. Instead, I would say that it is a direct social commentary on the flow of money and economic life as experienced in de La Tour's day. Issues of class and power are woven into the story of the old man's plight. The people of the Touraine region, particularly the craftsmen and laborers, were heavily taxed to support endless military efforts. But, the military and clergy (those with the power in those days) were exempt from such taxes, leaving the burden to fall on those who were the principal servants of the economy. So, in this story the old man is the middle-class everyman whose plight is exacerbated by the futility of taxing the poor and the self-serving protection of wealth and power by those with the "right" to tax.

Georges de La Tour was a careful dramatist, who understood the underlying human conditions created by the economic and political environment. His message is clear but not strident. His painting is not a judgment as much as a witnessing. He has portrayed the predicament of the craftsman as one in which

---

1. In *Georges de La Tour and His World*, Philip Conisbee (Ed.) presents the various ways to interpret this painting in a historical context.

this worker is stuck in the middle—as if in an eternal moment. There are no doors in the painting, no escape except through the eyes of the viewer. I can certainly empathize with the predicament, the tension, with the presence of power and the sense of doubt or worry, all of which are also part of the field created by the light.

The message of the painting also carries a kind of instruction. Each of us likely has all of the characters in the painting within ourselves. We can play every role in relation to money, depending on the circumstances—the taxpayer, the collector, the authority with power, and any of the cast of supporting characters as well. I am perfectly capable of shining that same pinpoint of light on my own interiority, but I also have to be willing to accept the shadows as part of the whole. In painting, as in life, both the light and the shadow, the *chiaroscuro*, are different sides of the same coin and share a common, and in this case pointed, source.

9. Money and the Dance of Death

Hans Holbein the Younger : *The Rich Man*

*T*otentanz or the Dance of Death was one of the most prevalent artistic and literary leitmotifs of fifteenth- and sixteenth-century Germany. The presence of death was visible everywhere in the culture because of the frequent occurrence of plague and other deadly diseases. One's longevity was uncertain: there was a sense that one could be visited by death at any moment. An artist always has choices in how he or she conveys a theme, the moment in time, the circumstances, and the setting. In a series of forty-plus illustrative woodcuts, Hans Holbein the Younger shows Death coming to people from all walks of life: beggars, priests, knights, and craftsmen.

The woodcut process itself demands precision and predetermination in its crafting, and thus every detail is significant and telling. Holbein chooses to personify Death as a character with just enough flesh and bones to animate its presence. No black cloak, no scythe. This Death has body language (contributing graphically to the quality of the dance). In this case, in gathering up the "Rych man's" money, Death is mirroring back to him the act and quality of the greed that led to such accumulation. It is a truth-telling and a mockery, a demonstration of the man's own shadow. Death has breached the thick-walled, iron-grated chamber, the rich man's inner sanctum. There are strong-boxes, money bags, and coins everywhere The room is cell-like, probably meant to be a protective vault; but now it looks more like a prison of the rich man's own making. The man protests, of course; he is inseparable from his money. It is his life, his identity. But, having put all his stock in the security of money, it is now his vulnerability.

As Hans Holbein makes it clear, in the realms of death and the spirit, money, and life have no security value. In no small linguistic turn misery is the external expression of the inner condition of the miser. It is the "immaterial" aspects—the rich man's connection to money, his relationship to it, and to the shadows he carries around it—that find expression in Death's appearance and the death process.

THE RICH MAN
Hans Holbein the Younger (1497–1543)

This is the story Hans Holbein tells. The candle on the table has burned down. The hour glass has run out. Death comes to collect the money, not because it has a use for it, but because it has a lesson to teach. The moment of destiny is non-negotiable. The consequence of greed and unabated accumulation of wealth is a legacy of false security.

Interestingly, art has the ability to transcend time, and it rises into and falls out of relevance in a rhythm sympathetic with our need to experience a truth that returns balance to the human sense of well-being. What was designed by Hans Holbein the Younger and printed to educate an audience in the sixteenth century seems relevant still, though today we seem to have less of a taste for moralizing. Imagine, if you will, this woodcut as propaganda for the so-called "death tax"!

USURER WITH A TEARFUL WOMAN

Gabriel Metsu (1629–1667)

10. Mercy in Mercantile Times

Gabriel Metsu : *Usurer with a Tearful Woman*

Seventeenth-century Dutch painters were devoted to painting scenes from everyday life, with all its drama, humor, and social dynamics. These genre paintings served as social commentary and, in some cases, were meant to deliver moral lessons. This certainly seems to be the case with this painting by Gabriel Metsu in which he has staged a scene that shows a forlorn woman in tears (handkerchief appropriately upstage) who has come to plead her case before a money lender or "usurer." In the foreground, her left hand holds the remnants of a document—probably a promissory note or other legal document. The money lender's face clearly indicates his scorn or judgment. One can easily surmise that there is a debt owed and not enough money to pay it. It is doubtful that this is the woman's own debt, given the monetary practices of the times. (Gender equity in the financial sphere is still an evolving ideal.) It is difficult to be precise about this painting, but perhaps it was the debt of her husband gone off to sea and not returned, as this was the time of the birth of mercantilism and international trade, which provided the primary cause of the growth of lending and borrowing and the amassing of wealth—and broken lives.

In keeping with the prevailing view of the time, usury was tolerated as a necessary evil (in the truest sense of the idiom). Metsu doesn't look favorably on either side of the transaction—the coldness of the money lender who can barely be bothered to look up at his client, the helplessness and vulnerability of the woman who has few other options. The usurer wears his cloak almost as a protection from her. But the painter's real point is made through subtleties and painterly devices. In the left background, behind the money lender's head, is a folded sheet of paper or canvas. On that surface is a portion of a face looking at the scene both with interest and some judgment. Whose face is this? It seems to have religious mood—possibly Jesus or John?—which sets a subliminal moral undertone in the painting. A more overt indication of the artist's perspective is in his use of light and shadow on the woman's purse. At first glance it looks as if a cloth or the liner has been pulled out of the bag. But it is no accident that the light catches it in such a way that it looks like a hand reaching into the bag. This surely is the artist's projection of his view of how the money lender operates.

It is interesting to me that Metsu's real attitudes and feelings about money and relational transactions were relegated to subsidiary details. To address them directly was taboo then, as it is now. Of course, the history of and attitudes about lending and borrowing have evolved since the seventeenth century. But, given the degree of consumer debt and the precarious state of the economy, I could imagine this scene playing out many times over in modern dress and on the telephone. One hopes the quality of mercy prevails.

11. Judas's Dilemma, Giotto's Rendition

In a small fresco panel, one of a series in the Scrovegni Chapel in Padua, Italy, Giotto painted Judas agreeing to betray his master in exchange for thirty silver coins. The sequential panels tell the familiar story.

In the garden of Gethsemane, Judas indicates Jesus by the kiss he gives him. Jesus is arrested and crucified according to Roman custom. Seeing the arrest, Judas is beset with guilt and tries to return the coins to the priests, but the priests refuse them.

Judas throws the coins onto the floor of the temple. They are recognized as "blood money," collected, and buried in the sinners' graveyard. In despair, Judas hangs himself.

Giotto portrays the scene of betrayal with the character of Satan standing behind and guiding Judas. One might say that Judas is serving as the agent for this shadow character, who is visible to the viewer but not to any of the other figures within the painting itself. Thus, we are the witnesses of Giotto's telling of the story, a perspective that indicates there are forces at work in the transaction which are beyond immediate human perception. Yet, they are all too human.

In Giotto's rendition, the shadow is Judas's own shadow. It is clearly attached solely to him. Though Giotto's rendering depicts the shadow as a physical character, Judas is the true actor, having internalized the shadow role he was to play. Logically, one would expect the satanic character to be present at the fulfillment of its wish. However, this is nowhere evident in the scene in which Judas kisses Jesus. It was not needed there because that force was

JUDAS RECEIVING PAYMENT FOR HIS BETRAYAL
Giotto di Bondone (1267–1336)

already foreshadowed in and contained within the promise Judas had made for the compensation he received.

According to the Bible, we know that Satan is an adversary of the Christ, but was unwilling to attack Christ directly. Satan (or Ahriman, which is another name for the same archetype) instead operated as much as possible through the agency of others and in the shadows, so to speak. Within this framework, we are witness to a double transaction, the work of Satan through Judas and the exchange of money for Judas's commitment or promise to the priests to act at a later date. This act of destiny changed the history of

Western consciousness through the process of the Crucifixion. An associative pattern, connected to and reflected in this moment, is buried within the Christian ethic—that money and the activities surrounding it are bad, or even evil, and likely to corrupt faith and the spirit. The phrase "filthy lucre" has its origins in this ethic.

Giotto is famous for having brought the art of representational rendering to a new level early in the Renaissance: his figures are not only columnar and dimensional, they also display their emotions and humanity. The Scrovegni Chapel was a very special venue for Giotto's frescos because he was responsible for designing and painting the entire chapel—a rare event in an artist's life, which provides us with an even rarer glimpse into an artist's genius. What emerges is his extraordinary capacity for storytelling, and in that storytelling, the revelation of insight.

In this small fresco of the betrayal, Giotto has portrayed one of the mysteries of money—he has demonstrated how intention is transmitted through a financial transaction. In accepting the money to betray Jesus, Judas was morally bound to the intentions of the priests, who, probably for political reasons, could not or would not directly identify Jesus themselves. Satan also had an intention aligned with the priests, but also could not act directly. The money itself was returned to the earth; it had served its purpose as a medium and transmitter of intention. By taking his own life, Judas was relieved of his physical body in time and space, and returned to the spirit.

While this highly Christian story casts aspersion on the act of financial transaction, it is also true that positive intentions can be conveyed through the same mechanism for the benefit of all parties involved. In its rightful place, money is a servant, not a tyrant. And every transaction is part of an unfolding story.

TEN DOLLAR BILL, 1956

Roy Lichtenstein (1923–1997)

12. Free Market Money in a Pop Iconomy

Whwhen Roy Lichtenstein first created his lithograph of the ten dollar bill, he was building a bridge between the highly idiosyncratic artistic vocabulary of Abstract Expressionism in the 1940s and 1950s and the emergent interest in an art of mundane objects of mass production and sensibility, such as money and comic books, in the 1960s. Another way of looking at it is this: Pop artists reversed the modernist tenet of "making the invisible visible" (Paul Klee)—which assumed the primacy of inner experience. Instead, they attached a certain aesthetic aura to common commercial and public imagery. In the optimism of the post-World War II U.S. economy, nothing was more prevalent in everyone's daily experience than the dollar bills that circulated, each with its cachet of consumer potential. When artists focus attention on and use as subject matter such a common and desirable object as money, it takes on a new meaning simply by asking viewers to take pause at their own experience of physical money. This subtle inflection-reflection in daily experience helps us to see it with new eyes, and to value its aesthetic as well as its purchasing power. No one would accuse Roy Lichtenstein of counterfeiting money. That was certainly not the point. Instead what we experience is his raising of the mundane to the status of icon.

Probably the best known and most controversial (though not the earliest) example of this "iconizing" was Andy Warhol's "Brillo Boxes" (1964) in which he replicated the existing commercial packaging and displayed his work alongside standard manufactured Brillo cartons. On one level, the two were indistinguishable. This was to a degree the demonstration of a philosophical

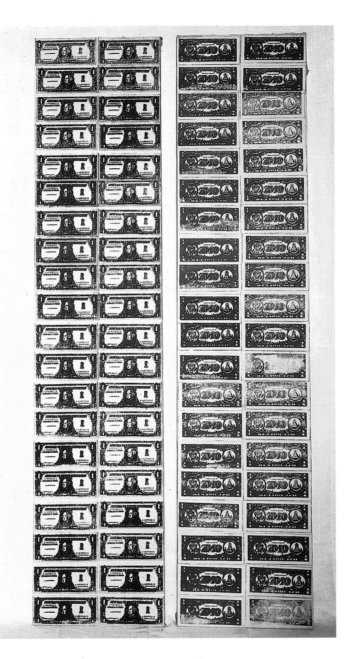

FRONT AND BACK DOLLAR BILLS

Andy Warhol (1928–1987)

proposition: What is the significance of the exercise of identifying the original from the replication when, in fact, they are both replications in the first place? The authority and presence of the artist's hand in the work, an association that goes all the way back to the early Renaissance, has been displaced by the presence of concept. It is no longer the making of the work or object of art that is important. For Warhol, this is a mechanical process. What becomes important is how the "work of art" is situated within the culture of common experience.

Warhol adopted the commercial photo-silkscreen process in 1962, which enabled him to generate and replicate images with great rapidity. Virtually anything could be photographed and reproduced, including existing images.

Among his work of 1962 are several that use the dollar bill as the source image. It may be an ironic twist of history that Andy Warhol's paintings and drawings of dollar bills were created the same year that Milton Friedman first published *Capitalism and Freedom*, the seminal book that framed the rationale for our current free market economy. In essence, Freidman's theory was that an economy operating free of governmental control would of itself raise everyone's standard of living. The conflation of freedom, in the democratic sense, with economic forces set up the culture for unfettered profiteering—what I would call the shadow rather than the supply side of capitalism. One unfortunate consequence of this economic philosophy is that the world of business and commerce has managed to control not only the marketplace, but also the rules and regulations governing those activities, such that the concept of a "level playing field" for economic opportunity is nothing more than a myth. Once upon a time, money was created as a system of values for accounting transactions; it was a means toward an end of the continuous circulation of money in order for everyone's needs to be met. However, in our free market economy, the endgame is money and accumulated wealth, a systematic reward for competitive behavior. The rights that are at the heart of political freedom, which protect equal economic opportunity and our common natural resources, have simply become more commodities available to the free market.

Thus the "almighty dollar" has taken on an iconic quality in which the representation and the ownership of it has overshadowed the underlying structure and value of what is represented by that dollar—and, of course, its real value is subject to change at a moment's notice. In order to feed free market activity, the government through the private agency of the Federal Reserve issues more money as it controls the supply and the interest cost of using it.

Both Lichtenstein and Warhol already recognized the luster of power that was attached to money in the early 1960s. That is why the representation of money could stand beside the representation of other commercial imagery—Marilyn Monroe and Campbell soup cans. By co-opting these popular images, artists, along with a host of others in the Pop Art movement, were paralleling the emergent free market economy with a free market of images. In the 1960s, I would say that that power attached to money was optimistic, possibly exuberant. Money was idolized. Warhol chose a medium of easy replication to generate his money paintings. Repetition of an image tends to attach a certain importance or meaning to it, even though replication ought to dilute value as the supply increases. He was deeply interested in the means of production; and, the fact that he was reproducing the image of money as a private citizen was also a challenge to the meaning of the government's right to do the same.

Though one cannot spend Warhol's dollars, they provide a reflection on the nature of cultural and expressional freedom in a way that practitioners of free markets could not understand because of their desire to control the rules. The curiously congruous timing of such seminal economic and artistic works in 1962 is the sign of an emerging consciousness at work, resulting in conflicting or complementary expressions. Would that art had the same power as Friedman's economic theory.

13. Money and the Modern Mind

What an invention money is —one of the evolving mysteries and wonders of the modern world. Among all the factors of everyday life, money and its attendant issues consume more of our conscious time than most of us would likely wish. It gathers about itself mythology, shadows, and power; and fear and greed seem to be ascendant driving forces everywhere. At least that is what the cultural media reflects, and perhaps fosters. Those who hold to generosity and compassion as principles are not often visible, and generally there is little reward for taking such a position. Yet, there is a growing cultural shift toward a positive direction.

That money seems so invested with power and control arises partially as a consequence of the fact that it is minted and issued by one central authority and, secondly, from the shadow cast over it by our culture and its history. The effects of this shadow are further amplified by unexamined archetypal forces, both good and bad, that remain in the subterranean constructs of our psyche. Indications of this unconscious reality tend to surface in unpredictable and often unexplainable ways. One need only reflect on working with money in a relationship or other social or organizational context.

Though it is desperately needed, there is not yet an easily accessible lexicon or other constructive expressive form free of cultural baggage to help bridge experience and communication around money. When one takes the time to look a little deeper into a conflict over finances, to explore the values and intentions, then the difficult personal situation or group dynamic can be dissipated or resolved. But this takes training and commitment—and time, rarely afforded in the hustle of everyday life. After all, these days most of our financial transactions are instantaneous and many are not even conducted with another human being.

Where are the opportunities to explore these deeply significant issues of money and the modern mind? Why does our culture hold such a long-standing taboo against talking about money? Where are the new lexicon and practices for disenfranchising this cultural taboo and healing our relationship to money? Who or what has withheld the permission for these conversations? And, why? Where is the resistance? What will create the leverage for long-term transformation for individuals and for culture?

Take the case of J.S.G. Boggs, a contemporary artist. Out of simple necessity and artistic mischievousness, Boggs began his money journey in a restaurant by drawing a $20 bill on a napkin—since he did not have money to pay for his food.[1] Mind you, he is an accomplished draftsman and the results of his work bear a remarkable resemblance to the real thing. His proposition goes as follows. When the waiter brought the bill for the meal, Boggs offered him his drawing of money as payment. Of course, that automatically put the waiter in a personal, philosophical, and financial quandary.

The condition that Boggs sets is that if the restaurant accepts his drawing as payment for the bill, they have to give him his change in dollars along with the receipt. He also requests the name and address of either the waiter or the manager, which he then writes on the receipt. Several things have been accomplished in this transaction. Boggs has had his meal, and he has generated all of the documents that will become the final work of art that surfaces in his gallery. The work of art as it is presented in its exhibition format consists of: the receipt from the restaurant, which documents the time, place, participants, and the cost of the transaction; the physical monetary change itself; and Boggs's original drawing, which either the gallery or a collector has taken the time to purchase from the individual who accepted it as payment in the first place.

---

1. For the full story and detailed analysis see Lawrence Weschler, *Boggs: A Comedy of Values*. University of Chicago Press: Chicago, 1999. The book also has an excellent bibliography on the cultural aspects of money.

TOP: J. S. G. Boggs, *Project: Pittsburgh* (1993). Back of a ten-dollar bill.
BOTTOM: Back of an actual U.S. ten-dollar bill

Boggs has traveled to many places and has learned to survive quite well on his own "currency." He has used it not only for food, but also for rent and clothing. In each case, the negotiation, process, and documentation conform to the conceptual framework he has practiced since the first restaurant experiment. The works all appear in his exhibitions and can be viewed on the web. To indicate how close to the legal edge of the acceptable his art and life take him, he became somewhat of a celebrity in England where he was tried and acquitted for counterfeiting British pound notes.

Boggs has also managed in his own tongue-in-cheek way to point out how we create value in our transactions, and just how attached we are to a monetary system that surrounds us everywhere, remains opaque, and over which we have little to no control. Boggs's actions penetrate to the deeper concept of value and further evidence just how functional, fictitious, and perception-based our normal unexamined monetary value system is.

There is something uplifting about knowing that someone has found a way to directly link his own creativity and authority through a social form that is parallel and complementary to the existing system. Mind you, Boggs asked for change in normal currency as a kind of proof and standard of value. It is also interesting to note that the "money" and other documents that are part of the transactions he has made have increased in equivalent value through the process—a remarkable reflection of the merits of a complementary or gift currency.

There is a modern fairy tale quality to Boggs's story in which he plays the trickster. However, venerable fairy tales, such as those collected by the Brothers Grimm, also offer insights into archetypal pictures associated with money. There are numerous stories from the Brothers Grimm that speak to the topic—stories such as "Star Money" and "Stolen Farthings"—but none address the full constellation of archetypes as well as an obscure story called "The Grave-Mound."[2] While this article does not allow space for the full story with the cadence of the language through which it is told, the characters themselves are instructive.

First and foremost is the wealthy farmer. While surveying his riches his eyes fall on the iron money chest in his sitting-room. Just at that moment there is a loud knock close by him. "The knock was not at the door of his room, but at the door of his heart." The door opens and a voice inquires about what good he has done with his money, what choices he has made between greed and generosity, for example. The farmer's heart is not slow in answering with the painful truth about his selfishness and hoarding.

Then there is a knock on the door to his room. It is a neighboring peasant whose children are starving. The peasant goes through all the fears and doubts about asking for a gift. The rich farmer intuitively recognizes the importance of this opportunity to begin his own rescue. He "looked at him [the peasant] long, and then the first sunbeam of mercy began to melt away a drop of the ice of greediness." The rich man gives the peasant more corn than he asked for with a

---

2. These stories can be found in *The Complete Grimm's Fairy Tales*. Pantheon Books: New York, 1944.

condition that he watch over his grave for three nights when he dies. The peasant agrees, and, of course, the farmer dies shortly afterward.

In fulfilling his obligation, the peasant meets two characters on the third night of his grave-watch. First he notices a stranger in the churchyard. "He was no longer young, had scars on his face, and his eyes looked sharply and eagerly around. He was entirely covered with an old cloak, and nothing was visible but his great riding-boots." In a state of anxiety, the peasant asks him who he is. "I am looking for nothing, and I am afraid of nothing!... I am nothing but a paid-off soldier." The peasant, recognizing the value of his company, invites him to keep watch with him. "To keep watch is a soldier's business. Whatever we fall in with here, whether it be good or bad, we will share it between us." The soldier agrees to this.

At midnight the "Devil" appears to claim the rich farmer's soul. He tries to scare off the peasant and the soldier to no avail. So the Devil changes strategies and "he thought to himself: Money is the best means with which to lay hold of these two vagabonds." The soldier considers and accepts the offer with the condition that the Devil fills up one of his boots with gold. The Devil goes off to get the gold. The soldier cuts the sole off his boot and places it over a hole in the ground close by the grave.

Three times the Devil has to go in search of ever-increasing amounts of gold. But each time he pours the gold, the boot remains unfilled. At some point the Devil realizes he has been had, but he has to keep to his agreement. After the last weighty sack has been poured in and the boot remains empty, the Devil becomes furious and is about to rip the boot from the earth. "At that moment the first ray of the rising sun broke forth." Unable to bear the sun, the Devil is forced to leave, and the farmer's soul is saved.

The conclusion of the story goes: "The peasant wished to divide the gold, but the soldier said: 'Give what falls to my lot to the poor, I will come with you to your cottage, and together we will rest and live in peace on what remains.'"

Each of these characters represents an archetype with a very particular relationship to money, the need for it, and its uses. While each of us may identify with a different character—who would willingly identify with the Devil?—we are home to all of them, for better or worse. Different ones come to the fore, depending on circumstances. What do we do with the wealth of our gifts, whether money or talents? Can we see the transformative and healing opportunities that recognizing and reconciling our own money shadows offer us? Are we open to listening to our hearts? Do we know how to ask for help without pre-judging those whom we are asking? Can we be completely free and without fears, and still be committed to service? Have we not used money to try to get our way? Can we honor our agreements, even if it takes us into the unknown and puts us at risk?

Just as Boggs has found a way to externalize his inner values through the modern money system and to point to a truth about money by inverting the system on itself, the archetypal pictures in the fairy tale offer an engaging tool, even a language, for exploring our own inner money landscapes, testing our assumptions, and understanding what is at play in our psyche. It is amazing and possibly unnerving to think of how the modern mind could come to know itself through bringing consciousness to bear on money—and that might begin to change the way the world works with money.

14. The Touchstone and the Labyrinth

A Step into the Mystery of Money

There are occasions when a mix of metaphors actually generates new meaning, though I was scolded often enough by my English teachers about the practice. In my recollection, they never mentioned that there might be value and meaning in understanding and finding language for a real spiritual world and my place in it as part of conventional discourse, as challenging as that might be. Of course, forgiveness is in order, since I was being taught at a time when science held objective knowledge of the material world as an article of faith. So, I learned to live with that myth along with the ongoing wonder and mystery of experience.

Paul Klee said that the purpose of the visual arts is "to make the invisible visible." From that pathway I have come to recognize money as a medium of expression, as a social technology, and one that also makes the invisible visible by bringing together value with material goods. Money taps as deeply into the human interior as it circulates widely about the world. While it is not a hard stretch to see that spirit and matter coalesce in nature, it is a more complicated proposition to see that spirit and matter coalesce in human nature. As a human invention and intervention money is an exemplar of and living laboratory for this play between interiority and exteriority—one aspect of spirit and matter. Money is linked to our material needs and our participation in economic life, and yet what it represents is entirely abstract, non-material and, to a degree, faith based. Value is thus a big player in the mystery drama of money.

A mystery is by definition enigmatic, and tracing back to the invisible from the visible is an exercise fraught with ambiguity. However, I hope that a step taken with humility may shed some light on the experience of money's mystery. This inquiry explores two ancient objects, the labyrinth and the touchstone. Both have come to serve as symbols of and metaphors for the physical and experiential aspect of money. The labyrinth hosts the personal pilgrimage, the journey one takes reflectively while moving through one's life path. The touchstone is used to measure the quality or purity of gold (as well as silver and other alloys) by applying dilutions of acid—the acid test, literally. Both objects denote material meaning and purpose, and both have come through connotation to be used as metaphors for experience. In combination they speak to me of the mystery, the inside-out, of money.

Those who have walked a labyrinth with an open heart know the power of the experience. Its path is a ritual journey from the threshold at the entrance to a more metaphoric threshold at the center—a path of discovery and self-knowledge. Walking the path, one feels part of some deep archetypal world filled with energetic and intuitional processes. Once at the center, one can travel no farther on the horizontal plane of the earth. Instead, the journey becomes vertical, traveling from the gravitation stillness of the feet on the earth and up through the uprightness of the spine toward the sky. It is on this vertical axis that one turns to commence the outward journey.

It is a beautiful and powerful moment, that merging of vertical and horizontal. It is a private journey in which my inner and outer self meet and through integration make meaning together. The center of the labyrinth is, in concentrated and magnified form, an imagination of many moments I experience each day as I move about the world, aware both of myself and myself in relation to others, through conversations and interactions as I and we. Such transactions (and I mean this in the highest sense) happen parallel to or across the plane of the earth. However, there is another element to a transaction, one that has a vertical quality. As one is in conversation with another, meaning arises (or descends, both vertical actions) out of mutual understanding. It is almost as if it transcends the two individuals present. This meaning is taken inward as it is transformed into understanding, and then outward as it moves to action. In a financial transaction, the third element, the meaning, so to speak, to the transaction is value. Again, it arises (or descends) at the moment of the transactional agreement, then disappears until such time as the object being traded is the

THE LABYRINTH AT LIFEBRIDGE SANCTUARY
Rosendale, New York

subject of another transaction. Thus, like language, money is both a medium of exchange (horizontal) and a measure of value (vertical)—a kind of mathematical metric of meaning.

The labyrinth is an ancient form found nearly everywhere in the world, across many cultures, and in many variations of design, scale, and formulation. The form is emblematic in and of itself, and serves as a framework for ritual; it is both container and contained, design and process. Labyrinths are remarkably simple—as are many archetypal forms—out of practical necessity. They were carved into stone as soft as sandstone and as hard as granite. These ancient petroglyphs look sometimes like a cosmic fingerprint, sometimes like a map of the human brain. Where they were constructed to be walked, they emanate an invitation to the journey.

Stone is a currency of labyrinths. Most are built with stone or stone tiles, thus each stone contributes to the energetic field of the form. The path of the labyrinth is one of consciousness, a spiritual journey bounded by the materiality of the mineral world. It is a fascinating relationship between the spiritual and the material; each requires the other to have a whole meaning. And, it is through the physical and metaphysical uprightness of the human being that both are recognized and realized as a confluence of nature and human nature.

As much as the mineral kingdom has provided the stones of our architecture, walls and ways, it has also provided veins of metals and crystalline stones that are deemed precious for their properties. Their perceived value has played out in complicated scenarios throughout history. Gold, of course, comes to mind. It has been mined from ancient times and has always had great value attached to it for its beauty, durability, stability, malleability, and rarity. The long-ago stolen capstones of the Egyptian pyramids were made of gold—gold placed at the intersection of earth and heaven, of the material and the spiritual. In Egypt, gold served as the emblematic representative of the power of the pharaoh, ruler over all things material and the only earthly embodiment of the spiritual world and the afterlife.

At the same time, in the Dead Sea and Mesopotamian regions, gold began to be used as the material of some of the earliest money because of the sacred power it retained, even as materialism was rising. Soon afterward, when different forms of metallic coinage came increasingly into use as a storage device for value in trade and exchange, a measure for the quality and purity of gold became necessary.

The storied touchstone, a stone of fine-grained schist or jasper, has a long history of use by assayers of the value and purity of gold. It was used as early as the fifth century BCE, and continues to be used to this day for the same purpose. The method is straightforward. The gold to be tested is swiped across the stone, next to one from gold of known purity. After an initial comparison, the test strip is lightly washed over with dilute acid, which dissolves impurities and alloy metals, but not the gold. Through a progression of increasingly concentrated acid, the quality of the gold is determined. This is the science of the touchstone. Its poetry is as a litmus test or standard bearer of quality or tone, a metaphoric benchmark of value.

Both the touchstone and the labyrinth have a sense of ritual about them, ritual processes leading to revelation of outer value and inner worth, an alignment of the outer and inner. They serve well in harmony to characterize some of the archetypal aspects of the money mystery.

But money has changed in recent years. It has become much less connected to the human experience as exemplified by the touchstone and the labyrinth. Just as we may be coming to a place of understanding something of its mystery by exploring the world of stones, its physical and metaphysical aspects, money has essentially jettisoned all physicality. It has been reduced to electronic pulse, a pure currency that moves invisibly and speedily. Our bank accounts are mere way stations, and our on-line accounts and ATM machines nothing more than meters for the comings and goings, credits and debits. There is no relevant test for the purity of the medium of exchange, and no time to journey with it through transactions. The touchstone and the labyrinth are about real experiential value, much as money has been throughout its history.

Recent currency has no real value, no reference point as found with the touchstone. We live, instead, with fiat currency which means that it has no standard or reference tied to the mineral world, or otherwise. The United States officially left the gold standard in 1971 under President Nixon. Today's money is simply made legal by governmental decree, meaning that it is actually a fiction declared as fact. So I am left with the questions: Post the experiential and metaphoric relevance of the touchstone and the labyrinth, post a material basis for money itself, how do we go about understanding money in relation to the human psyche? Where, or even how, does money reside in the mystery of the human being? What tools and senses are needed when the work at hand is no longer about making the invisible visible? Instead, what seems at work in the impenetrability of Wall Street transactions, such as sub-prime loans and other "exotic" financial instruments, is keeping the invisible *invisible*. The process for this is to use the language of visibility and count on the habit of continued belief in its truth, because it may be too painful and disruptive to do otherwise.

Hans Christian Andersen's fairy tale "The Emperor's New Clothes" comes to mind, in which all the wisest counselors and courtiers convince the king that the new robes being made for him are magnificent, even though they do not actually exist at all. Of course, in Andersen's story, it takes the voice of an innocent child to call out the truth in public and to lift the veil of illusion from the emperor's eyes.

Though there seems no need for a touchstone to measure the quality of our coin, to test our mettle, so to speak, the essence of the labyrinthine journey may be more important than ever. As money is increasingly reduced to nano units and moves ever faster, it will become increasingly indistinguishable from the rest of our experiences in the world. For example, there will be less time to exercise the kinds of choices that are now the privilege of the conscious consumer. The moment of purchase could be almost simultaneous with the thought of the purchase. Thus, the spiritual self we come to know through the journey, with all its gifts and foibles, desires and needs, will be completely visible in the economic self that buys, sells, invests, and gives. We may already be there; but we are still able to operate under the cloak of rationalized invisibility. Where is that innocent child's voice? And, when will we hear it?

15. The Transcendentalist and the Immigrant

Two Views of Money in America

The desire for money as a tool of culture was implanted in the American consciousness early in its history when Alexander Hamilton held sway over Thomas Jefferson in setting the economic direction for the future. Simply put, Jefferson argued for a land-based (or agriculture) economy. Hamilton was a monetarist. In Jefferson's framework, the land and America's abundant natural resources, if properly stewarded, would provide for a sustainable economy. But Jefferson, as a land and slave holder, was also an architect of private owner-ship, along with other framers of the constitution. In many ways these positions set up continual conflict between private ownership and the concept of the commons, which holds that natural resources are held by all with right of use as the economic element.

Hamilton's vision of economic trade required a monetary system as a tool of accounting to accommodate intra- and inter-national exchange of goods and currencies. His approach presumed that all things physical could be mone-tized—labor and natural resources as well as commodities. This monetarist approach explains the generation of great wealth (of the monetary sort) through the consumption of nature. Hamilton, along with international counterparts, set the groundwork for financial innovation that has transformed money from a physical substance minted and held in treasuries (the gold standard and Fort Knox) to an almost purely electronic record (most money these days is actually generated by the banks as debt).

Much more could be addressed concerning the economic dynamics broadly identified here; I mention them primarily as background for two other perspectives on money in America that speak more to the direct human experience of what has resulted from Hamilton's policy. Ralph Waldo Emerson (the American transcendentalist) and Eva Hoffman (a Polish immigrant, who moved to Canada at age thirteen, and then to America) offer exemplary insights into and voices for the culture of money that has evolved in America. Emerson wrote the essay "Wealth" in 1860. Hoffman's book *Lost in Translation: Life in a New Language*, written in 1989, is about her impressions of our modern American culture.

These two voices evoke a moral tone that sounds across time. Though each of the insights is inevitably seated in a historical moment, a deeper theme emerges and resonates in new expressions. Though American culture looks very different now than in the nineteenth century, the quest for a moral understanding of money, its purposes and its effects on the human condition, remains. Consider the following passages by Emerson and Hoffman, written more than a century apart, which address money and the American experience from a moral perspective in surprising ways. Emerson forewarns us of the moral challenge of accumulating wealth. Hoffman, the modern and open-hearted immigrant, witnesses the force that money bears, and sees only two paths of recourse to its pressures.

Here is Emerson:

Whilst it is each man's interest, that, not only ease and convenience of living, but also wealth or surplus product should exist somewhere, it need not be in his hands. Often it is very undesirable to him. Goethe said well, "nobody should be rich but those who understand it." Some men are born to own, and can animate all their possessions. Others cannot: their owning is not graceful; seems to be a compromise of their character; they seem to steal their own dividends. They should own who can administer; not they who hoard and conceal; not they who, the greater proprietors they are, are only the greater beggars, but they whose work carves out work for more, opens a path for all. For he is the rich man in whom the people are rich, and he is the poor man in whom the people are poor.

And, Hoffman:

The gospel of detachment is as well suited to a culture of excess as it is to a society of radical poverty. It thrives in circumstances in which one's wants are dangerous because they are surely going to be deprived—or because they are pulled in so many directions that they pose a threat to the integrity, the unity of one's self....Money, in America, is a force so extreme as to become a religious force, a confusing deity, which demands either idolatry or a spiritual education.

It is quite clear that Emerson, a preacher and deep interpreter of the Anglo-Saxon, Protestant American experience, was heralding the force of money at work in the culture of the early nineteenth century, and already experiencing the effects of it himself as a member of the contribution-supported clergy. He could see that land holders, bankers, and emerging industrialists were accumulating wealth through the right of ownership of land and capital. The first sentence of his passage establishes wealth or money as necessary to the well-being of humanity, but questions the right ownership of that wealth. He is in some sense positing wealth as part of the commons. His primary inquiry then was into the question: Who should be given the right of the use and distribution of that wealth?

Emerson was a student of human character—surveying its inner aspects through exploring the soul and linking that capacity to the higher, more transcendent forces of the spirit. He also understood that a person's character, or essence, has a greater effect on one's own behavior and on the surrounding community than any measurable capacity of intellect. (See: Emerson's lecture "The American Scholar" given to the Phi Beta Kappa Society at Harvard University, 1837). But he takes character analysis another step by looking at whether wealth is owned selfishly or on behalf of others. He is clearly in favor of an altruistic (on-behalf-of) rather than ego-centric practice. Charles Dickens's Scrooge could be considered an exemplar of both inner and outer transformation from "stealing his own dividends" to "carving out work for more," from greed and fear to generosity and compassion.

Emerson took the sense of land stewardship described by Jefferson and applied it to the monetarist model. In other words, he recognized that wealth or money had become the new "natural resource." But he does not directly answer the question of how it could be determined who is a good administrator. He counts upon the individual's own highest moral integrity to self-determine if one can administer on his terms. This is truly the transcendentalist speaking—that a human being can rise to the higher self in order to hear the reflective voice of truth as affirmation or condemnation of her or his practice of social responsibility. There is a kind of inspiring idealism in this imagination, and ample demonstration of good practice in the philanthropic sector. It is not an accident, but rather an integral part of its character that America, for all its flaws, far surpasses any other country in its charitable generosity. In some ways, Emerson presaged the evolution of public charities in America (from their origins in the community chest of early seventeenth-century England) as trustees and administrators of wealth for public benefit.

In his time, Emerson could not have known the extent of the wealth that would be generated first by the industrial revolution, and then the technological revolution. He did not imagine that wealth generation would be separated from direct work, investment, or natural resources. But that has happened. Much wealth, though certainly not all, becomes self-generating via indirect investment through public stock trading, hedge funds, and other such well-orchestrated financial instruments. Financiers and wealth advisors have become the new priesthood, confessors, holders of family secrets, and cross-generational shepherds.

Such is the presence and power of money in the modern American economic landscape that a young, impressionable person stepping into it brand-new might realize the moral dilemma and choices it presents. Eva Hoffman writes from such a vantage point, but her message is not like Emerson's. Hers is a depersonalized one in which the personal—one's identity—is defined not by a sense of self as it was for Emerson, but rather imposed on the individual by the confluence of material and cultural circumstances. According to her narrative, the external pressures of the melting pot separate one's self from one's deeper, authentic soul experience and sense of community.

One can see this in the effect that contemporary media and marketing have on the identity formation of young people. Were I to succumb to this effect, I would think of myself as a brand rather than a self, an image rather than its source. This is the disconnection that Hoffman uses as her framework. In this light, one can hardly know the sources of desire or wants. Are they, for example, part of some image of myself subtly created by someone else's commercial agenda to get me to buy a product that I may not really need? The passage brilliantly alludes to the connection between virtual or invented desires and the virtual wealth created by an overheated consumer and investment culture. They thrive on each other. Hoffman sees the causal relationship between the creation of wealth and the rise of poverty. Those in poverty will never have enough; those with wealth will face a multiplicity of choices and never-ending demands to spend.

Hoffman observed the power and attraction that a culture of everything-for-sale had on her attention. Purchase takes on the mantle of ritual. Desire is connected to the worldly and material, rather than the spiritual. Value resides in gratification, not celebration. Money devolves into the icon of this experience. It comes and goes; its sheer impermanence, presence, and absence create fluctuations in one's emotional life that are a far cry from the constancy of faith one might have in a higher being. The idolatry she speaks of is that of the biblical golden calf in which the thing itself, its material presence, is the locus of connection and belief. The antidote to such a materialist practice is a spiritual education that cultivates deeper human values and reverence for the mystery and generative principles of life—the spiritual, which lies within or behind the material. Hoffman argues that this spiritual perspective and the practice of its values protect the self from the illusory power of money and all that it represents of a purely materialistic world view. Her ability to articulate this important distinction is based upon the strength of her soul-rich childhood experiences weighed against the pull of her new cultural experiences.

Both Emerson and Hoffman were aware of the dynamic duality of the spiritual and the material. Emerson recognized it as an integral part of his philosophical framework, which had its heritage in a cultural thread from Aristotle and Plato to the science and spirit of Goethe. He came to understand and influence human experience through this wisdom. Hoffman came to her view from direct and personal experience, through the struggle to survive as a transplant in American soil. On the topic of money, Emerson's transcendentalism is matched by Hoffman's intuitive intelligence and her ability to engage us in her reflective process. Where Emerson instructs, Hoffman invites us into a modern dilemma: the capacity of money to dis-integrate inner and outer experience. She proposes two paths, two pathologies, but leaves us free to choose, maybe to bargain. Both authors were deeply engaged with the American experience and the American soul as witnesses and participants. Both ask us to explore our relationship with money as an instructive reflection of our soul, and possibly that of our broader economic life, as uncertain and highly abstract as it is. Both courageously call for a level of moral consideration of money that is often lacking or ignored in American discourse and culture.

PART II

A Topography of Transactions

1. Economics and the Presence of Philanthropy

Imagine what our world would be like without the presence of philanthropy. Certainly, we would continue to produce and consume. We would continue to save or invest any surplus generated out of basic economic activity, and likely, investments would continue to grow and be reinvested. The "economy" would continue to grow. At the same time, organizations that depend upon gift support and volunteer time would suffer, unless they became somehow profitable. Any activity or service with a purpose or end that is other than producing a profit—such as education, research, and the arts—would basically be headed for extinction. The conventional economist might acknowledge the social consequences of this, but register no economic ones. This is why it should come as no surprise that philanthropy, the art and science of giving, is not to be found in classic economics text books.

As one of the primary means of support for education, or any field connected with renewing the human spirit, philanthropists know that philanthropically-funded activities actually have a very important place in the economic cycle, from a social as well as economic standpoint. Philanthropic gifts are generative in nature. That is, without charitable gifts there would be no economic activity at all. Proof: In the history of humankind, gifting processes have notably preceded all other forms of economic trade transactions and monetary systems, and societies found ways to meet all the basic human needs without any monetary systems at all. In addition to physical needs, such as food and shelter, these economies valued the non-commodity aspects that conventional economics cannot fathom, like caring, learning, imagining, inspiring. Yet these are the very things that really matter most to us day-to-day. But such intangibles fall outside the quantifiable world of modern social science. They are nice, but not economic. Rather, it has been left to philanthropy, which is primarily motivated by these intangibles, to make whole the fragmented and generally inhuman picture of economics. Given this encompassing perspective, I would posit that gifting is the most important and productive component of an economic system.

In the world of risk and return, a gift is 100% risk, while the returns on the gift are immeasurable—so rich are they in the experiential and qualitative aspects of life, so laden with potential for the future. The fascinating thing is that charitable activities are actually structured to consume, even burn up, excess capital. Through this transformative process, they produce new human capacity (education), new insights and breakthroughs (research), and cultural innovation (the arts), all of which often lead to economic renewal. It should come as no surprise that these three areas (and there are others, of course) are primarily supported by gifts and taxation, a form of mandatory gifts.

Philanthropists know that accumulated capital is the most vital source of gifting. Money "ages," becomes more disconnected from human initiative as it accumulates. As soon as that money is given away it leaves the sphere of investment and is given new economic life by being used for purchase to accomplish a charitable mission by the recipient. Thus the linkage is established between the generation of surplus capital and the renewal of that capital through philanthropy. The logic here is one of functional integration rather than cause and effect. Historically, philanthropy is something you are privileged to do because of your financial success. This may be considered a nineteenth-century industrial model, but that, too, is shifting. More corporations and individuals are structuring their philanthropy as part of their present financial activity rather than putting it off, pending the results of a career. For example, the dramatic increase in young people's interest in philanthropic activity is a result of activism and engagement; they want to make a difference with their lives now rather than viewing the accumulation of resources as a measure of accomplishment. This sense of social responsibility and integration is but one reflection of a much larger, though now just barely visible, sea change in the emerging field of social finance.

Social finance holds that the purpose of money and finance is to support human initiative and to foster the evolution of new communities. Social finance recognizes that in the context of a global economy, we are fully interdependent. It is no longer possible to stand outside this reality, regardless of political boundaries, accumulated wealth, or dire poverty. Social finance recognizes the human and environmental consequences of economic activities. In this paradigm, for example, socially responsible businesses are capable of bringing about needed changes in our culture through fair labor practices and the charitable distribution of a portion of their profits. This is just one emergent approach in which gifting is integral to the whole economic cycle. It presents a picture of a healthier sustainable future—and one that leaves behind the industrialist model of philanthropy which lives so strongly in the mythology of American history.

2. A Window into Transparency

The Desire for Connection through Finance

I have a friend who began his career in the Netherlands at a small family bank that had relationships with clients going back some two-hundred-plus years. He once saw a balance sheet from the bank's earliest years in the eighteenth century, and found the name of a trading firm that is still a client. This is truly a long-term relationship—an unlikely scenario in today's banking and finance world. His assessment of the continuity and success of the financial relationship: the trust and accountability that comes of living in the same community, seeing each other at the marketplace, and the awareness that failing to pay a loan could have consequences for neighbors and the local economy.

This story came to mind because recently I read an article in *The New York Times* (July 19, 2008, B1, B6), under the "Your Money" section, titled "When the Banker Knows Your Mother" by Ron Lieber. The article is an inquiry into the value of community banking in the face of recent banking disasters, such as the failure of IndyMac in Pasadena, and the disconnected and impersonal aspects of purely on-line banking. The article indicated that the challenge for local banks is to match the interest rates of their more space-based than place-based competitors. But, risk is also an issue. When the president of Easton Bank & Trust, a community bank, was asked about the risk to his bank he replied, "The first loss we take here is my personal loss. It's my personal equity in the bank, my personal reputation in a community I've lived in most of my life. I'm not just dealing with other people's money, so it's a whole different level of responsibility." In the opaque, distant, and mostly digital world of current finance, this kind of thinking and the willingness to take personal and community responsibility strikes a harmonious chord in my heart, and also bespeaks social and community values that offset "advantageous" interest.

Risk and money, especially when it is my money, opens up a host of questions around tolerance, desire, greed, and, hopefully, higher social purposes. In this vulnerable state, transparency of intention and action operate as a tonic, as does access to knowing the people with whom I have entrusted my money and their ethics. Transparency is a window into the other side of financial transactions. Current risk-reward models run the gamut from casino-like high risk, high reward hedge funds and derivatives to simple, low interest, no-risk insured savings accounts. The story is always based on the assumed validity of the risk-reward model as motivation for material gain. In fact, we have developed a whole rationale around risk and reward that basically rewards—even celebrates—risk and treats reward as a compensation for having given up other uses of the capital.

In the venture capital model, the investor is tying his or her fortune to the success of the entrepreneur; while the entrepreneur, in some (but not all) cases, is likely working toward exit strategy or buy out, yet another form of reward. The end goal of all this risk-reward activity is the generation and extraction of capital from the economic process. One positive aspect of the venture capital model is that investing is actually directly in the project and the work itself. It is based upon the faith that the investor has in the success of the undertaking and the abilities of the entrepreneur. Transparency is inherent in this structure, as it is in many ways a co-creative process between the funders and entrepreneur, at least at the outset. However, this cohesion is ruptured, for example, when the company goes public and its shares are traded for their perceived value—that is, the next round of investors are paying the original investors for the shares. Little or none of that money goes directly into the company itself. At this moment the risk-reward model is disengaged from any real value and is delivered into the prestidigitation of being publicly traded on Wall Street.

In an economic world that turns on self-interest, the calculated risk sits with the owner of the money. As a result of this self-interested imperative, investment and kindred financial activities have gone from enabling new capacities on the part of entrepreneurs (direct investment) to extracting capital from the capital system itself (indirect investment). Extraction is the means, accumulation the end. The concentration of wealth has another significant effect: restriction of the flow of useful money. Money that could bring about cultural renewal and innovation is instead tied up in real estate and other material goods.

One could read this as a judgment of wealth. It is not. Wealth is critically important to everyone, though it may feel different or in fact *be* different depending upon one's perception and cultural norms. This is, however, an argument in favor of circulation rather than accumulation, of direct transaction rather than indirect transaction, and of transparency rather than the impenetrability and weight of Wall Street, which is so perceptively revealed in this photograph taken in 1915 by Paul Strand.

WALL STREET 1915
Paul Strand (1890–1976)

Easton Bank & Trust is one example of a more human-scale, localized financial organization—a model of money serving community through real relationships. In many ways, credit unions and cooperative banks share this quality of community and accessibility. However, there is another economic form that addresses the question of risk in a deeply social and innovative way. It is neither banking nor investment, but rather it is a community-centered financing structure, as direct, personal, and transparent as imaginable. By its very nature, it is designed to support, indeed assure, a vocation along with production and distribution of goods, free of the adverse competitive pressures of the marketplace. There is no betting; and the risk-reward model is turned inside-out and upside-down. The model, as practiced in the United States, is called community supported agriculture (CSA). About twenty-five years ago, the first such economic association was started on the East Coast of the U.S., having been previously implemented in Northern Europe. Today there are well over two thousand such groups in operation, though not all are equally true to the original associative intention.

The concept of community supported agriculture is transferrable to other contexts, and in fact has been applied to medical practices as well. But, for clarity, I will describe it as applied to community farming. First and foremost the farmer identifies, develops, or adopts a community that is interested in connecting with the farm, the farmer's values and practices, and the joy of being a partner in the economic life of the farm. Then, the farmer determines how much food can be grown, and thus how many families can be fed from a seasonal output. Based on the number of shares that can be grown, the farmer puts together an annual budget that encompasses all of the farm activities, including the purchasing of seeds, equipment, and health insurance, farm maintenance, and living costs for the whole year (not just the growing season). In the interest of engagement and transparency, the farmer may even invite members of the community to participate in the formation of the budget. This total budget is then divided by the number of shares to arrive at the cost per share. The "price" is thus arrived at in an associative manner in the sense that all the parties to setting the price have brought their needs and perspectives into the process—somewhat akin to fair trade practices.

The benefits to this process are many. The social and community ones are self-evident. However, the economic advantages bear further discussion for what they represent as the opposite of the opaque world of conventional finance and pricing schema. First, the farmer is free to farm as he or she best knows how, without the pressures of the market-based competitive economy, or the demand for the return of capital. Second, because there is a direct connection between the farmer and the shareholders, there is no middle distribution or wholesale system to add to the cost, or reduce what the farmer receives. The most interesting part of all, and the part that takes the most education for those new to it, is that the risk of farm or crop failure is shared across the entire community. The shareholders pay the cost for the farmer to farm for the year, and they receive food as a by-product, say seven months out of the year. If there is a drought one year, or some blight, the farmer is still supported by the share income, and will be able to farm another season. The shareholders bear the risk. In a bounteous year, the shareholders share the abundance. What this means is that the shareholders are not consumers in opposition to a producer; rather, they are co-producers. Neither are they paying in any direct way for the food or treating the farmer's labor as a commodity. The beauty is that the farmer's livelihood is not subject to the vagaries of market forces and the rising tide of climate chaos.

In the CSA model, risk and reward are actually separated from each other and reconfigured to support the vocation of the farmer. In conventional investing, reward and risk are linked through input and output in the money system. The borrower or investee uses money for production and leverages the marketplace to repay the investor. In the community-supported system, the point of the entrepreneur (farmer) is not one of economic gain, but rather of sustainability, and a mission to heal the earth and cultivate soil fertility. This interest in matters beyond self-interest permeates the associative form and raises the commitment of community members to also rise above self-interest.

CSA is an associative community-centered financing model that needs no corporate or legal structure to operate. It is instead, a self-governing economic community that determines its agreements in light of the needs of the farmers and the members. In some sense, "enoughness" and sustainability are built into the model, and the money simply serves this end. This is also a completely transparent, personal, and direct form of economic relationship that has a localized base and a capacity for self-renewal. I would hope for and imagine that all economic activity will someday operate within this associative approach—though scale will always be a challenge. Associating in this modality meets the rising need to connect in community through finances in a very simple and immediate way. It is a picture of the future of economic activity that returns money to its role as a means toward local and sustainable community.

That *The New York Times* would publish an article addressing the value of the local and the personal in the context of "Your Money" is significant. It points to not only a rising need for connection, but also the legitimacy of deeply human relational values that are the foundation of trust, which is precisely what has been betrayed by the recent financial and banking disasters. Thus, any financial form that fosters transparency is to be celebrated for the healing it brings to our economic consciousness.

3. Just Money and Social Finance

Money is a source of great pleasure and pain. How it is used both heals and harms individuals and societies. But, money is not a thing. It is symbolic. It serves a broader and deeper economic system, embedded with rights, values, and intentions. On a simple level, money was invented to account for value in the production and exchange of goods and services. Such an accounting system inevitably reflects the values, priorities, and flows of human activities. Dig a little into the system, whether your checkbook or a national budget, and you will find a mirror of your economic self or the character of a national economy. Through financial transactions, expenditures and revenues, you will see what you, or a country, really care about. Dig deeper, and you may awaken an awareness of what was created and sacrificed of human and natural resources in order to make those transactions possible. Dig deeper again, and you will see a hyperkinetic field of money, currencies and material that transcends political boundaries. In our current global economy, the circulation in this field is permeated with greed and "never-enoughness," which generates enough friction to overheat our societies and environment.

This brilliant accounting system we call money has been corrupted and exchanged for a profit-driven endgame of control over natural resources and human manufacture. At the center of this exchange are the functions of debt and interest. Debt, of course, makes it possible to start enterprises and own homes. The mutual interest of the lender and the borrower in each other's success is a central tenet of social finance, an approach to finance that places primacy on social benefit in financial affairs. Lending and borrowing have gone on for millennia imbued with culture-specific values and mores. But interest charged for debt is another matter all together. What first served as a system of compensation for "giving up the money" for a time became a system of compensation for an absence of trust or "risk mitigation." While both of these approaches to interest continue to be at play, the demand for immediate financial return on money and the rapid increase in predatory lending practices on a local and global scale have turned financing and debt creation into an extractive industry—extracting wealth out of the seemingly limitless supply of debt. Debt and interest have become the tools for creating wealth while increasing poverty—though many who control the wealth would not frame it that way.

Only a small and privileged percentage of the world's population can define their economic lives in terms such as investing, saving, or consumer choice. Those who control wealth have abrogated the right of ownership by imposing the right of use through raw financial power or the ability to control policy and law. Water, a basic necessity, is a glaring example of this. Water has existential but not economic value until it is transformed through production into a commodity. By this logic there can be no private right of ownership of water, only a right to use it, granted by those who own it in common. Claimed "economic rights" are enforced primarily for the purpose of the control of production and the creation of wealth, not for stewardship and sustainability. This example of natural resource appropriation is symptomatic of having lost sight of the original and higher purpose of economic life—making sure that the physical needs of all human beings are sufficiently met in order for them to be contributing members of society. This is the economic base of a free society. But, economic life is simply not simple.

There is increasing awareness of the injustice and corruption of our current global money system, and increasing attention is being paid to innovative economic systems that respect human dignity and the social value of local economies and currencies. But changing the destructive patterns of over-consumption, over-production, and degradation of community and environment will require concerted and sustained action, including transforming how we work with money in purchasing, investments, and philanthropy.

Throughout history, the darkest of times have spawned enlightened innovation. The same power of consciousness that gave rise to money and money systems is fully capable of thinking new thoughts when it recognizes that the present-future is grim without radical change. As we become more conscious economic citizens and realize how deeply interdependent we are, the social reality of finance will become not only more palpable but also more desirable. The principle of altruism—working to meet the needs of others in trust that others are working to meet mine—will replace the current driving forces of self-interest and accumulation.

The successful emergence of fair trade practices and certification is one outward manifestation of redirecting economic systems to more just and associative ones. Such practices include the voices and needs of all parties in the economic process from farmer to consumer. For example, international fair trade has taken over an increasing share of the coffee market and is expanding to other foods as well. Consumers are willing to pay more for the product because they understand the value and values in the transactions. On a more local level, the rapid growth of community supported agriculture around the world indicates that consumers want to participate in the economic life of the land, farmer, and food. In this model, shareholders divide the total annual cost of the farm with the result that the farmer will be supported regardless of the amount of food grown. "Community supported" also means a community of shared risk. Though this is a purchase model, it has a parallel in the field of micro-loans pioneered by Grameen Bank. This approach allows small loans to enterprising individuals who are part of a guarantee community. This group of peer-guarantors assumes responsibility for the success of their colleagues, such that the others will guarantee them when they have a need for an investment. This simple, powerful form fosters individual initiative, economic collaboration, and community building.

Conventional currencies are issued by centralized authorities, such as a government bank. As soon as this money is issued either someone or some institution owes interest on it to pay for its use. This triggers the inhumane debt-interest cycle. However, in recent years, complementary currencies and other leveraged currencies have been developed and implemented as a way to engage and enliven local economies, and to demonstrate that a community can create its own agreements around its value and use. The basic concept of a complementary currency is to facilitate a link between unused resources and unmet needs. These currencies circulate as a true accounting system as people meet each others' needs within the system's jurisdiction. Such a concept could include critical aspects of life, such as companionship or managing a home, which are not normally considered to have economic value. In some ways complementary currencies are harbingers of a true gift economy. What is awakened through them is an awareness of the needs of others and a capacity to meet those needs outside the conventional money system. Imagine a whole economy operating and no "money"! There are many complementary currencies active around the world, and they are increasing rapidly as local solutions to the global monetary crisis. Time Banks and BerkShares are two examples in the United States, and much more can be found internationally. Along with the growth of complementary currencies has come the concept of leveraged currencies such as Interra, which allows members to collectively allocate profits from transactions across the economic community of producers, suppliers, and consumers, toward charitable programs and community projects.

At its heart, money and its many forms are tools to empower each of us to improve the quality of local and global economic life. Without recognizing our inextricable connection to the whole world through our economic lives, to our dependence on others' capacities—whether growing food, making clothes, or educating children—we miss an important and daily opportunity to connect more deeply with ourselves and to work in whatever way possible to practice social finance toward a more just economy.

4. Consuming Identity

Iengage daily in purchase transactions. These range from food to gasoline, clothes, and airline tickets. For each transaction I have numerous choices to make—one of the advantages and challenges of living in a resource-rich, market-based economy. None of this is news. Each time I make a purchase—exercise my choice—I am acting out of my personal and social values. This transaction sends a message into the economic and production systems that encourages them to produce another item just like the one I have purchased. By being ever more conscious in my buying choices—for instance, by becoming increasingly discriminating in the sources of the materials or the fairness of the labor practices involved and being willing to pay for those qualities and practices—I am bringing my values to bear on the economic system. At the same time I constantly remind myself that such a frame of reference is extremely privileged, and available to a limited set of the world's population. The element of change I can bring about through such transactions is nanometric, but valuable nonetheless. This is the story I tell myself.

This story, however, has had others help write it. Cultural conditioning, class bias, inherited and unexamined values, media exposure, and my own instinctive desires all play a part in its crafting. This part I can own. This is *who* I am as a consumer, an evolving aspect of my identity. However, there are others who make it their business to usurp that authorship by overwriting or overriding that identity. The intention through advertising and other forms of commercial-based media messaging is to relocate my awareness from my ever-emerging who to *what* I am as a consumer. That is: to objectify myself, to condition what I see as I reflect upon myself, as if the image in the mirror is the end of the reflective process. After all, an image is a thing, and we are very image-conscious.

Consider the following from the *Art Directors Club Annual No. 34* of 1955: "It is now the business of advertising to manufacture customers in the comfort of their own homes." "To manufacture customers"—what a dehumanizing and impossible imperative. What a misapplication of the industrial mind-set. And yet it was an overarching and brilliant strategy to control and commodify self-perception. In some ways, the very notion of personal spiritual or cultural freedom, that part of myself that I consider most sacred and inviolable, is put at risk here by an intention to redefine it as solely economic and dependent. According to this advertising imperative, I am only me in relation to the material world and what I buy or own, and more insidiously, to some fabricated projection of how I ought to be.

The year 1955 was a watershed year for the commercial world that emerged post-World War II. That year televisions numbered 30.7 million and were owned by fifty percent of the population. Three years later, there were more TVs than people, homes, or cars. For a quick context: 1955 was the year that MacDonald's and Disneyland opened in a hail of optimism about the future; "Queen for a Day," an early form of what we now call reality or tabloid television, began broadcasting; the first atomic reactor began generating power in Schenectady, NY; the first bus boycotts began in Montgomery, Alabama; and "Rock Around the Clock" (a telling title for our time) was one of the most popular songs. This is just to mention a few cultural signposts.

While 1955 was certainly not the beginning of the advertising industry, the new media of TV opened up vastly increased opportunities for persuasion. The industry has become what I consider a place of genius (if understood for what it is) for concatenating sophisticated understanding of the human psyche, pathways for influencing it, and the use of communication tools to effect that influence. The precedent for advertising lies in propaganda; its deepest shadow was already known as "brainwashing." It is an industry of people highly sensitive to cultural currents who recognize no limits to inventively co-opting what is deeply human in me and in my relationship to others and the world as a tool for further objectifying my "self" as an image—all the while maintaining the illusion of real experience. I would suggest this is true for each of us depending on how we relate to cultural identity or the degree to which we share in a collective unconscious filled with archetypes having different names but common characteristics.

There is nothing simpler, more direct, and engaging for people than storytelling. It is an ancient art, a living art of communing with our fellow humans. Storytelling is an efficient means for experiencing authentic voice. I intuitively experience someone's truth (or untruth) as they tell me their story, whether biography, recollection, or fiction. I also experience my own truth or untruth as I tell my story; storytelling has powerful reflective capacities. Interestingly, storytelling is having a significant comeback in Western culture as a way of reclaiming that voice so polluted by cultural messaging systems. I imagine that you can probably guess the most recent trend in the advertising industry—the use of storytelling because of its assumed authenticity, its ability to convince or engage.

A historical precedent for this twisting of veracity was the innovative use of photographs in print ads in the 1920s. Photographs replaced illustrations because the new medium supposedly told the truth ("cameras don't lie" was the theory), while illustrations were no longer convincing. We have come to understand that cameras do "lie" and that photographs are alterable representations, so much so that they are no longer accepted as evidence in court. Ethical practice aside, this is the way the advertising industry goes.

As a consumer, I live in the rift between who I am based on self-knowledge and what the world of commerce is trying to make of me based on self-image. While a purchase transaction is nothing more than an exchange of value, there are other layers of meaning that play out through it. The story that compels me to the purchase, including a dose of self-interest, whether driven by legitimate or imagined need, interfaces with the product's or service's story, including what and how I was made aware of it and what it is trying to say about me. Sometimes the stories mesh nicely, other times not. I experience a degree of both dissonance and integration emerging within almost every transaction I make. Being awake to those feelings, which constitute the soul of the transaction, is a step beyond conscious choice in consumerism and toward returning "who I am" as I author my story and "what I am" according to others to their appropriate domains. This is, of course, a powerful and sacred exercise in individual freedom and a central challenge for our time.

5. Real Virtuality

QQ Coins and the Quandary of Complementary Mercantilism

Coincidental emergence occurs when a new system or structure surfaces alongside its originating system. Often this emergent world coexists as a complement to the original rather than as a replacement for it, much as an afterimage arises from a color. The conventional approach to explaining this phenomenon—for instance, that I see green as an afterimage of red—is to rationalize the secondary system by cause and effect. However, once this emergent world is understood to have its own reality, its own rules, and its own function, the causal relationship is no longer relevant. The postmodern world is filled with such emergent virtual worlds: image is mistaken for the thing itself; simulacra abound; we think we are communicating through the internet, when in fact we are messaging; we transact business through credit cards and ATMs, and call it money. Names for things are designed to create the illusion of the familiar and known, when the facts contradict the implied connection. A complementary color is only an opposite in a world defined by polarities. The virtue of reality is that the world doesn't really operate that way. It is multivalent, both-and, complex, and in constant movement through time.

Cause and effect are loosely linked through non-rational as well as rational dimensions. If one follows through in the experience of an afterimage color, the afterimage itself has an afterimage, which in turn has an afterimage—each image a transformation of its predecessor. The color of origin becomes a distant memory, but the experience of each emergent image is just as valid as the original sensory one. By exploring coincidental emergences and by understanding their "unconventional" logics, the apparent rational and "conventional" world can become clearer.

In this frame of mind, I read a fascinating article in the *Wall Street Journal* (March 30, 2007) entitled "QQ: China's New Coin of the Realm?" written by Geoffrey A. Fowler and Juying Qin with contributions by Lina Yoon. The story is about QQ coins, an online virtual currency originally issued by the Chinese company Tencent Holdings Ltd. (an intentionally ironic name?) for users of its instant messaging system ICQ to "purchase" virtual flowers and other such niceties to send to correspondents. As with other virtual currencies used in video games, the virtual coinage serves as an incentive and has value so long as it stays within the boundaries of its own system. Any accumulated earnings can only be used up within the system. For me, the simplest example of this is playing a pinball machine and "winning" an extra ball or new game.

The crux of the *Wall Street Journal* story, as they reported it, goes like this: "Then last year something happened that Tencent hadn't originally planned. Online game sites beyond Tencent started accepting QQ coins as payment." In other words, the rules of one "virtuality" were co-opted by another "virtuality." The QQ coins crossed the boundary of one system into another with a different though somewhat parallel set of rules. The authors cite the convenience of managing and accounting for petty transactions online as one of the primary motivations for the shift. Interestingly enough, other online game companies recognized the essential value of the virtual QQ coins. Like real money they represent nothing more than an accounting system for which Tencent already had a structure that could be leveraged for the sake of efficiency. This is free market mercantilism at its best.

But the QQ situation quickly became more complicated. The subheader for the article reads, "Officials Try to Crack Down As Fake Online Currency Is Traded for Real Money." The article spends much of its focus on the quandary the Chinese Government is currently facing. One result of free market mercantilism is that it can quickly generate a surplus. The article goes on to state: "At informal online currency marketplaces, thousands of users helped turn the QQ coins back into cash by selling them at a discount…Traders began jumping into the QQ coin market as an opportunity to make a quick yuan off of currency speculation." Yet the authors never question how "real" the real currency is. Of course, once the QQ coins were pegged to conventional currency value, they could be used as a parallel system for real commodity purchases beyond the reach of government control and the tax system. And, with the advent of secondary exchange markets, transactions related to QQ coins can occur both within and between the virtual and real money worlds. The Virtual Economy Research Network [virtual-economy.org] calls these transactions of conventional currency for virtual property RMT's or Real Money Trade.

Back to the pinball machine model. Provided the pinball game is online, there is now a mechanism to sell that extra game to someone else for an agreed upon price. That person can then use that game either to play online, or to sell for cash to someone else who wants to use it, or thinks it can be sold again for more. One can see very quickly how many schemes could unfold. The article mentions a few, such as "intimate private chats online" and online gambling. For a government used to tight regulation, the open market and economically democratic invention of the online virtual world is a challenge.

One notable difference between conventional currency (yuan) issued by the government and the QQ coins issued by Tencent Holdings is their physical versus virtual realities. They are both monetary systems that stand in for an accounting of value, at least until they are sold as commodities. The government sets the value of the yuan, and, since the government stands in for the people, it represents, for better or worse, an agreement by which the citizens abide. What supports the value of the virtual currency is not just the supply and demand, as the authors of the article state, but also the quality of perception and what the currency makes possible. QQ coins came into existence in order to enhance online communication, to add emotional value to an instant message. As superficial as that may appear, it is the motivating human emotion that makes the virtuality of the coins real. For a user to be able to operate in an "economic" life free of government control is itself a coincidental emergence.

Many virtual currencies are part of or attached to online games. And there is an aftermarket in RMT to purchase some of the virtual equipment used to play those games. One need only explore eBay to find them. This kind of trade is driven by the desire to profit from a willing market. It is based on the flawed assumption that what is virtual is real, like mistaking the image for the thing itself. The fictional Wizard of Oz was, of course, one of the modern masters of this kind of illusion. His power lasted until the curtain was pulled back by Toto and he was revealed to be manipulating the machinery of deception, and all too human in his humiliation. But Oz was a dream from which Dorothy could awaken.

Virtual coins and virtual realities are not dreams, they are complementary systems that first emerged as a mechanical reflection of human consciousness. As a result, they exist as a kind of afterimage, alternating between the light and shadow of that consciousness. The Chinese Government has every right to concern itself with the QQ coins and their potential for creating economic chaos. The government's goal would be to return QQ coins to their own self-contained system and thus sever any linkage with the conventional system. The real interest is in controlling the value of the "coin of the realm" by also controlling the perception that that value is controlled. What the QQ coins point out is that value is a spontaneous occurrence, and is drawn into currency by perceived need, convenience, and reduction of hindrances to the flow of human activity.

Tencent Holdings probably never imagined that QQ coins would flow over their intended boundaries. But neither does the company have an interest in stemming the flow. Tencent gains visibility and publicity as it demonstrates that a currency is only as vital as its social and economic efficacy. There are thousands of complementary currencies at work in the world, solving important social problems that governments may not recognize as having economic interest or have the resources to meet. Where currencies arise out of a community's interest, they tend not to compete with, but rather augment or fill the void of conventional currency. Where currencies are issued by for-profits to leverage their businesses, they will inevitably compete with governmental currency when those currencies become commodities. Open market or exchange currencies, as Tencent's QQ coins, are designed not only for competition, but also to capitalize on market-based efficiencies, which leverage existing resources such as the yuan. What threatens any government is losing the authority or control over the emergent self-governing power of this profitable currency. But then the legal issues governing virtual online activities are yet another dilemma—whether the current body of national and international laws apply to a virtual world. The complement or afterimage of law would be chaos, because an absence of law would be socially inconceivable. In the case of QQ coins, chaos, at least, has real virtuality.

6. A Degenerative and Regenerative Economics of Philanthropy and Gift

One of the mysterious characteristics of a gift is that it increases in value when it is received. Value is, of course, a multilayered phenomenon and a complicated subject, but it can also be simple, personal, and direct. Suppose it is winter, and you have an infrequently-worn warm coat in your closet. If you were to give that coat to someone who has none, then the value of that coat has increased drastically because of its increased usefulness, regardless of its original cost or sentimental value. Value actually requires a transaction in order to be realized, yet the perspective from which it is viewed remains relative—to feelings, perceptions, and historical context.

Something else important is happening within this transactional picture. The coat was hanging in a closet, out of circulation you could say, maybe even in cold storage or mothballs. Once given, it is now moving about in the world, providing bodily warmth and helping someone focus on their life tasks instead of the condition of being cold. Most important, this picture presumes a kind of ideal world in which the human being is valued more highly than material goods.

Money, especially gift money, works in a similar way. Money, which has been heavily or continuously used either for purchase or investment, or held in "cold storage" such as land or real estate where its primary purpose is an increase in monetary value, needs to be recirculated into the economy through gifts to support research, education, and other activities that foster human capacity for cultural renewal and envisioning the future. And, in its purest form, this renewal is done without any expectation of monetary return (though there may be a tax benefit). Where money makes possible the furtherance of human capacity, money is given, in a sense, a new life. Its value has increased for the benefit of culture and humanity rather than for the benefit of its giver.

There is a secondary aspect of this gift transaction that is equally important. That is, how the gift is received. A gift usually comes with an intention. If the recipient acknowledges the intention, feels responsible to it, then the recipient has, in a sense, met the giver on his or her destiny path. In this act, a spiritual link is created, like a bridge, between the past and the future. The receiver is taking on work that the donor recognizes as important and has resources to support, but has chosen not to do. This link between donor and recipient is also a critical part of the increased value of the gift, a transformation from monetary or trade value to human value.

While philanthropy primarily is concerned with giving from accumulated or surplus capital or time, a gift economy focuses more broadly on the circulation of gifts and assumes an ever-renewing human capacity for adding resources to that circulation—whether in material form such as goods, or spiritual form such as ideas. Philanthropy is a subset of the gift economy, but it is based upon the capitalist-based assumption that wealth or capital rightly accrues to the one or ones best able to organize human labor in economic activities. Thus philanthropy is made possible through an extractive and accumulative process. Historically it has been the role of philanthropy to return some portion of this surplus to the culture for public benefit, or to what English law called, in the seventeenth century, the "community chest." While it may not be treated as such in conventional economic thinking, philanthropy is an essential part of economic life when viewed through the qualitative aspect of financial transactions.

However, we live in and by another economy, which lies outside economic discipline, namely, that of caring, thinking, and relationships, among others, all of which we need in order to survive, but which also have no "economic" value. These human processes are the essence of a gift economy, though philanthropy is one element of it. While goods may be circulated as part of the gift economy, it is the recognition and celebration of human needs that serve as prime motivators—in other words, we are moved by a sense of brotherhood and sisterhood rather than self-interest. That the value of a gift increases over time is a modern mystery in that, while a gifted object or money gets consumed, the values that pass through the transaction do not. Instead, when one values someone that person's sense of value increases. In this view, the material and the spiritual aspects part ways to circulate in degenerative (material) and regenerative (spiritual) economic pathways. The reality is that we need both aspects, but we lack a science of regenerative economics to complement prevailing materialistic economic science.

7. Culture—for the Price of Admission

Ever wonder what exactly you are buying when you purchase a ticket to the symphony (or any other cultural event)? What appears as a very simple transaction becomes complicated when you begin to explore what you get for that "purchase." When you buy a car, there is a clear exchange of value—money for goods; when you hire a lawyer, the exchange is for a service. This holds true for the symphony as well. It is a service. But, the motivation, the real value, is in the ephemeral experience, transcendent or otherwise.

When you buy a ticket, you are purchasing the right to be in a particular seat on a particular day to hear a published program. That same ticket provides no other rights, unless, for example, there is a rescheduling due to rain. The ticket does *not* provide a right to expect or hear a brilliant performance, only the right to be present for it.

From an economic standpoint, the cost of the ticket is your share of the financial support needed to enable the philharmonic service to continue to be provided to the wider community. After all, the concert hall needs to be built and maintained, and the conductor and musicians need to be paid in order to bring their considerable gifts to rehearsals and performances. Your ticket purchase provides for the physical (earthly) needs of the orchestra as your need to attend for aesthetic pleasure is being met.

It is fair to assume that expectations come with the purchase, especially if the orchestra has a great reputation. Given your right to attend the performance and given that the musicians will perform, it is a sure bet that you will have an experience; but, the ticket purchase cannot guaranty the quality of that experience. Instead, the terms, value, and meaning are determined solely by you. How you absorb the music and carry it in memory into the future is particular to your biography. The quality of the experience, what happens *performa*, is in the nature of a gift. It is certainly not a thing; it is the result of a transpersonal (performers-audience) event. It defies any conventional economic measurement since the performance is simultaneous and nearly congruent in space for the whole audience, yet its effects operate outside of time and space for each individual present.

The price of admission to a cultural event is complex since the end of the transaction is not really economic, but rather experiential or spiritual, if you will. One test of this is to observe how much gift money must be raised to meet the true cost of operating the symphony orchestra. If the true cost were reflected in the price of admission, very few people would be able to afford to attend, and thus, lame the broader cultural value of the performance and the mission of the music. However much one winces at the cost of attending a performance, the ticket at least guarantees you the right to attend and provides for both your and the orchestra's economic needs. Rather than a charge against your income, the expense is to be celebrated as a gift in support of music and culture.

8. Toward a Topography of Financial Transactions

Part I — Prologue

My money-self, or that part of me that transacts with money, does not seem to be the same self that experiences the transcendence of music or poetry, or searches for social justice in daily affairs. This awareness indicates a rupture in the integrity of my inner landscape that I no longer find acceptable. Unfortunately, my culturally conditioned self urges me not to look into that ruptured space or past the edges of my consciousness in a way that might lead me to a deeper awareness of money and the social realities of finance. Yet, I am now compelled to work toward a kind of unified aesthetic which recognizes and incorporates that rupture, one that welcomes my money-self as an integral part of my inner landscape.

I propose that this ruptured condition around money is reinforced by the history and sociology of an invented and intelligent system that favors efficiency over equity, competition over collaboration. These aspects of the money system, especially, have a formative and profound influence on anyone touched by them, and certainly on me. In exploring and mapping my inner processes, I expect to unearth and reframe the desires, drives and needs that constitute my money-self as it expresses itself in me and through my actions.

Part II — Learning Money Messages

As a young child, I was unfettered by money and financial transactions. However, by the time I got a little older, the consumer world with its assumptions was already a fact and factor of daily life. From early childhood, money was disconnected from my natural learning process, except perhaps through imitative play. I was not likely to learn about it through a self-directed process of discovery, as one does in learning to read, for example. In reading, language has a cultural base that provides access to its roots in human speech and subsequent transformations as a tool of human relations. With money, the rules dictated a whole numeric value system that allowed me to learn to count and account but not to tap into expression and meaning. Value was a result of a dispassionate and objective process. Values, which represented what I really cared about, were never brought into relation with value. I have a vivid childhood memory that makes this disconnection clear. All the understanding of money and accounting in the world could not alleviate or explain the intensity of my feelings when I saw an open over-packed transport truck of orange-grove workers when my family was lost on a back road in Florida. We were on vacation and I had the distinct sense that we were not supposed to be where we were, and that I was not supposed to be seeing what I saw. I was nine years old. I can still see those faces staring at me, at us. The standing workers looked exhausted and swayed with the movement of the truck. My parents could not have known the deep impression that experience had on me, how it would feed a life inquiry into how a human being is valued, rather than just counted.

For better or worse, like most children, I lived in a sea of unspoken or received assumptions about values built into daily experience. The origin of meaning for money was absent, or at least it seemed that way. One clear message I ingested was that money is neutral, that it is nothing but what we project onto it (and a host of other psychological conditions). From a purely materialist perspective, that statement seems true. But, as I have come to see money as a creation and extension of the human psyche, and as a function under the control of government, I have come to think otherwise. The money system itself has and is the meaning. Buried within all the objectivity, measurement, and quantification, is the genius and tyranny of human invention—the very same human capacity that created both slavery and the Enlightenment; that understands and values the commons and commonwealth, while fighting vindictively over intellectual property; that exercises freedom in artistic expression, yet demonstrates an undiminished will to control nature.

As a child I connected deeply to the natural world. However, money is not of the natural world, or even evolved from the world of nature, though it has always depended upon some material, marker, or substance as its representative.[1] These physical aspects are simple measures of abstract concepts such as value, price, and wages—concepts defined seemingly irrationally or in the instant of a transaction. When I buy a new car, for example, it drops in value the minute I drive it off the lot. Or, consider the unsound idea that one can set an objective basis for compensating labor, although it is not a thing or a commodity. These are normal human economic activities with an unnatural monetary system imposed on them.

Part III — A Topography of Transactions

I am proposing here re-imagining a topography of transactions based on my desire and need to understand money and the powerful effect it has on my life. How can I begin to transform something as abstract and potent as money without first recognizing what I have been conditioned to assume about it? Then maybe I can understand how my financial behavior is governed by those unconscious attitudes, needs, and desires absorbed in my youth and is still active today.

There are several layers and conditions to any money transaction. First, it takes at least two parties with an agreement, even if unconscious, to bring it about. Then, there are the aspects of time and function, that is, the purpose of the transaction. These factors determine the transaction's nature and qualities, the particulars of which I will explore after first looking into the transactional elements that are common to all.

With any financial transaction there is a physical dimension to it, whether that is an exchange of documents, paper, coins, the swipe of a card, or a handshake.

---

1. Bernard Lietaer and Steven Belgin have thought deeply about money and argue cogently that it arises from agreements, and represents an agreement rather than being a thing. From a different vantage point, they are also saying that agreements do not exist in nature, but rather are a human innovation. An engaging definition of money can be found in their book, *Of Human Wealth: Beyond Greed and Scarcity* (Galley Edition V3.0), pp. 19–22.

This physical quality also happens at a moment in time and is accountable in a direct and measurable way. If one can imagine a world in which many such physical transactions are occurring simultaneously and continuously, and that the same physical objects (coin, paper, etc.) circulate through and across many such moments, then a picture of an energetic transactional field emerges, a field in which we all participate. We are creators of, and in turn are supported by, this circulation. By extension, this is an imagination of a fully global and inter-dependent economics.

Value is a highly subjective and perception-driven factor, yet it is a very real experience. I depend upon that experience continuously as I negotiate my financial path through the day. This experience is generated within my feel-ing life, even if at the level of a "hunch." How do I know there is value, even before I assess it? What constitutes something worth financial consideration? The intention to bring consciousness to a transaction depends upon this quality of knowing through instinct, feeling, or soul-sense. Based upon it, I can assess the perceived value in relationship to my personal values.

To recap, in each transaction there are four simultaneous, stratified yet inter-woven components—the physical, the participatory or circulatory, the qual-ity of feeling, and consciousness or recognition. Taken in the aggregate, each transaction has both measurable and more or less public aspects, as well as deeply personal and individual ones. From a social financial perspective this is important. Just as quantum physicists can measure the effect the observer has on the field observed, my inner condition affects the social quality of the financial transactional field. These non-material aspects happen all the time in our transactions, but we have little support and few tools for reckoning with them—and the assumption is that they have no economic value. The result is that we have a sub-rosa economy of intentions moving about the world along with money—possibly having greater long-term impact on the deeply human energetic level than the money itself.

This core-sample view of a money transaction becomes evident by drilling down into the transaction at the moment it occurs. However, transactions live in a much broader context of time and space, a context hinted at in the circula-tory layer. First, there are the day-to-day transactions through which I meet my basic needs. These tend to fall in the arena of purchase or an exchange of goods or services for fair monetary value.[2] This activity is expressly physical in nature and is driven primarily by my senses, needs, or desires. The moment of purchase happens almost instantaneously and, therefore, in the present.

Looking at the transaction strata, I would venture to say that purchases are motivated by or originate in the physical, as does the resultant circulatory layer. Value and consciousness are also present, but it takes inner work to bring these into the foreground. My experience tells me that progress toward consciousness is possible in these two realms, but it is a path full of compromise. For instance, though I know the environmental, economic, and political story of fossil fuels, I still find myself driving because of convenience or efficiency, when I might walk or take public transportation. For me, this awareness is only a step toward fully conscious actions.

When I look at taking out a loan, several additional factors emerge. First, a loan (or credit) hopefully has a longer time frame and larger purpose than a purchase, though a loan often makes a purchase possible. There is usually an agreement that defines the terms no matter how simple or complex—specifically, the cost of the use of the money (interest) and the time frame over which the loan will be paid back. What this means is that the parties to the agreement find themselves in a long-term relationship in which each has a stake in the success of the other. A loan, like a purchase, is driven by a physical need, but that need is usually for something that has a longer use life such as a house or car, or for a means of production that will leverage the repayment. In all these cases, the loan refers to an event (or purchase) that happened in the past. The perceived value of the transaction has to be weighed carefully, and trust has to be established and maintained by the partners to the loan. In this situation, the value stratum is very much in the foreground. Loans and investments enable new ideas to be brought into economic production. Consciousness pertains to seeing the connection between the value provided to the world through the investment and the expectation of financial and social return that motivated the

---

2. I am indebted to Rudolf Steiner for his articulation of the different qualities of purchase, loan and gift money. He described these concepts in his collection of lectures, *Economics: The World as One Economy*, Lecture 6, "True Price," p. 88.

investment in the first place—a dynamic tension between community interest and self-interest.

As much as investments are driven by this dual interest, gifts and the philanthropic spirit are motivated by interest of a different kind—of the human aspirational variety. The impulse to donate originates in consciousness. While there is a legitimate need to be met, it is not usually my need. Instead, the charitable need comes from the world toward me, and it is my awareness of that need that starts my philanthropic process. This process moves from recognition, to valuation, then to the physical gift.

Recognition and consciousness do not operate in the quantifiable frameworks of clocks and accounting. And, neither does a gift itself, really. A gift is given with no expectation of any goods or services in return. It is then used to bring about a charitable mission or the development of new capacities, the effects of which improve the condition of the world. To set a time frame for the outcome is an artificial construct. For example, if I make a gift to my child's school, I support the educational process, but cannot know how, when, if, or in what form that experience will become a capacity that directly benefits the world. My conclusion from this is that a gift operates into the future for the needs of others.

A topography of transactions has both inner space and outer manifestations. The strata of physical, circulatory, value, and consciousness are embedded in a time structure of past, present, and future. When the strata and time structure are overlaid, the resulting matrix becomes a topographic chart of my multi-faceted experience of the complex invention we call money and my transactional behavior with it. As money moves about the world at ever increasing speeds, used and abused, accumulated and released, I know at least that I can bring some consciousness to bear upon it and my participation in its circulation through transactions. Like the wonder connected to my discovery of reading, this article is my attempt to reclaim the wonder that lies buried in the human invention of money—through transaction to connection, to consciousness— and to release some of the fear and mythology that money has accrued. In the end, financial transactions are human transactions. They point to the reality of our interdependence, to the agreements within which we operate, and to the possibility for imparting warmth of consciousness and love through our participation in the circulation of money.

9. Faith, Hope, and Love

Elements of an Appreciative Economy

I said to my soul, be still, and wait without hope.

For hope would be hope for the wrong thing; wait without love

For love would be love of the wrong thing; there is yet faith

But faith and the love and the hope are all in the waiting.

Wait without thought, for you are not ready for thought:

So the darkness shall be the light, and the stillness the dancing.

—T.S. Eliot, *Four Quartets*

INTRODUCTION

My economic behavior is governed by many things—mine and others' needs, desires, available resources and products, social value, and moral and ethical currents, to name a few. Much depends upon my presence of mind, how much I can slow my inner processes down to evaluate the circumstances, my strength to assess the source of desire, resist where I should, and then understand the reality of how one pays for the transaction, whether credit, cash, or other means of exchange. Imagine, if you will, all these transactions happening in an appreciative economy, one that values the warmth of recognition, inspiration, and relationships, supported rather than driven by economic activity. In an appreciative economy, money makes compassion more economically feasible than greed.

Financial transactions constitute a subset of broader economic activity. They are elements in the landscape of exchange. They have their qualities, which I will explore from the perspectives of faith, hope, and love—not terms we normally associate with money. In the passage above from *Four Quartets*, T. S. Eliot situates these concept-percepts in the soul as part of an inner dialogue: "I said to my soul…" They are connected to each other, yet each has its own characteristic gesture. I am motivated to engage in financial transactions for many of the reasons indicated. But, not all financial transactions are alike. For example, the same dollar can be used for a purchase, a loan, or a gift. Each use or function is distinguished by the degree of attention I pay to relationship and time. Just as the soul gestures of faith, hope, and love are distinct from each other, so too are the archetypal qualities of those transactions. And the two are connected as I experience them. By understanding how the archetypal qualities and their soul gestures are active in financial transactions, it is my hope to offer some inner reflective tools for bringing more consciousness to money and its uses toward an evolving appreciative economy.

Faith

What do I mean by faith? The word denotes religious practices, but I would like to frame it from the perspective of a quality of soul. What is behind faith? And, how is it constructed such that I can recognize its presence regardless of a specific outer form or expression? First, my assessment is that faith, if not simply presumed by tradition, is built upon a complex of outer and inner inquiries and experiences over time. One superficial example is how one develops faith in a brand product. The first encounter is with the product and what the manufacturer and advertisers "promise" about how it will perform. That message is then either confirmed or contradicted by my experience of the product. Over time, I no longer have to evaluate whether or not I want to buy the product. If my experience continually confirms the promise, the product has earned my loyalty and thus my faith in its value. The selection of that particular product is now part of my habit life, and of course makes my shopping time more efficient.

The point is that faith develops over time. It has an inherent historical framework and usually a point of reference, such as a body of religious knowledge or a consumer need. These two kinds of faith are quite different in their degree of depth and the power they hold. Brand allegiance is not all that deep, or there would not be so much money spent on maintaining it. By contrast, imagine casually suggesting to someone that they change their religion. Religion has a body of knowledge, values, and practices with such a cultural and historical reach that this could be considered a form of cell or tissue memory, a kind of atavistic presence that reaches well into the past.

Loan transactions share something of this historical aspect in the sense that I take a loan in order to accomplish something, such as purchase a house, for example, and then pay for the use of those funds over time—whatever the agreement established at the time. While I am writing the monthly check in the present, the true reference is to the historical event. Hopefully, as part of the loan origination, there was a great deal of due diligence done on the part of both parties to the transaction. I would want to know who is lending me the money, what the exact terms of the agreement are, and what the remedies are, should they be needed. And the lender would likely be asking me about my creditworthiness, my financial history, where I work and how much I make, etc. The purpose of this "dance" is to validate the history and intentions of the borrower (what I will do with the money), and to determine, based on that historical picture, whether or not the future will be consistent enough with that history in order to assure the success of the loan. In other words, does the lender have faith enough in me and the activity I want to finance to make the loan? And, do I as a borrower have enough faith in my ability to honor my loan commitment?

Loan transactions are based on faith, regardless of how objective the loan process may appear.

Hope

When I say that I hope for something—someone's good health, or for something to happen—I am projecting an intention out into the future. Hope is future bearing. To attach specific outcomes or a time frame to it changes it from hope into an expectation. And, I have a different relationship to each, though I am not always clear in conveying which one I am actually inwardly holding. Pure hope is nothing but an open-ended imagination that may inspire me or others, but leaves me or others free to act upon that hope or not. After all, it is my hope, not theirs. This inner freedom is not of the political sort; it has nothing to do with rights or agreements. Instead, it arises from a spiritual, moral, or ethical place, which only I can access or know for myself. Therefore, if I listen to my own hope and decide to realize it through my own volition, I have made a commitment or agreement with myself. It moves from hope to duty. Those who respond to my stated hope also enter this same process for themselves. While it may be quite gratifying for me, I also have to realize that I have no control over the another person's process. They have taken it up out of their own inner freedom and for their own reasons.

Thus, hope has a deeply philanthropic aspect to it. When I make a financial gift, say to a charity, it only becomes a gift because I have given up any control of the money. If the gift comes with expectations or restrictions, it is still a gift but not a truly free one. The standard acknowledgment line, which states that you have received no goods or services in return for the gift, is a simple expression of this deeper principle. One might say that a gift has a spiritual value in reciprocity for the sacrifice of any material value. (Tax benefits aside!)

The aspect of freedom is paramount for a gift. If I make a gift based on an intention and in freedom, and it is received in freedom and with recognition of that intention, then something quite new has happened in the realm of transactions—a kind of destiny moment in which two parties are aligned, but totally out of free choice.

And, the true gift aspect of a gift tends to operate outside the rational basis of time. When I make a gift to a charity, that gift is usually quickly transformed into purchase by the charity—to pay salaries or rent, buy equipment, or whatever. However, the gift element remains in the capacity of the charity to benefit lives. This aspect cannot be predicted. In educating a child, one does not know what capacity that individual will bring to the world, or when it may emerge. However, it is pretty likely that the educational process itself can be credited with having contributed to building that capacity. In this way, a gift is entirely future bearing.

Gift transactions are based on hope regardless of the level of negotiation and agreement it might take to secure the gift.

Love

Just the thought of trying to delimit love as a soul capacity seems daunting. Love is one of those overly sentimentalized terms and everyone has his or her associations connected with it, for better or worse. Despite the frequent and demotic use of the term—Robert Indiana's memorializing sculptural form and its use in scoring tennis games come to mind—love has endured because of its deep significance for our survival as a species. The Greek philosophers worked hard at identifying some of its many aspects from the physical to the spiritual, and teasing out its rightful place in our consciousness and the qualities of our relationships.

Love is so central to my well being, so critical to the buoyancy of my life, that its presence is ever-present. And in a way that is just the point. Love and the practice of love are relatively meaningless except in the present. Love is the tool by which I fully engage in the world and know what is coming toward me from the world, sometimes long before I can make sense of that knowing in my head. The practice of love also generates an energetic field around me that unconsciously interacts and exchanges with others. Love is essentially connected with our being rather than our doing. It is a capacity of feeling that helps us to be awake to and be interested in others and their needs. Because it is so linked with my presence, I should not, in the ideal, need to summon it as a force from some shadowed depths. It is instead a matter of my being awake to it as it speaks through my decisions and actions.

Thus, when I am making purchases, exchanging money for goods or services, it is neither faith nor hope that is qualitatively present, but rather, love. Purchases have no historical or future reference. The value is solely in the equality of exchange at the time. As I know only too well when reselling something, the value may be very different in the next exchange. In contrast to loans and gifts, purchases happen very quickly and often in isolation. If I were to slow any of them down, all the variables that made that transaction possible might come into view: the thinking that went into the creation of the product; the labor that went into its production; the market that made it available; the vendor actually selling it; then, the need that I have; the work that went into earning the money to make the purchase; my values...and so on.

Suddenly, the purchase exchange represents the whole of our interdependent economic life encapsulated in one moment. There are potential challenges in this process. Because as a typical consumer I am seeking a good deal, I would have to be blind to the consequences of cheap labor, externalized costs, and environmental damage that allowed the price to be so low. If I were to slow down some purchases, I might actually be awakened to the mistreatment of people and animals that made such an advantageous price possible. I would be confronted with the discrepancy between my espoused values and how I practice them. If I am really paying attention to my authentic voice that actually knows and practices out of love, I would have to reconsider the purchase, and maybe not even make it. Love arises from taking a deep interest in the reality I create for myself, from the empathic attention I pay to the needs of others, and from my ability to actively forgive what might otherwise feel like an insult coming toward me.

As I use money to purchase material goods to meet my needs, I am being informed more or less consciously by a part of my constitution formed during my infancy, one might say pre-consciously. By this statement, I mean that at birth we are fully dependent upon our mothers (or surrogates) for our nurturance and nutrition. The quality of feeling that was connected with that process on the parent's part—the joy, the stress—are experienced as an associated part of the nurturance and thus become an integral part of our economic self. On one hand, this could seem absurd, on the other, it might help us to understand why money and how we use it, especially in the realm of purchase, is such a mystery to us, why we do not like to talk about it, and why it brings up all sorts of issues, particularly around the concept of what is enough. What need is really being met as we purchase to meet our needs (or, dare I say it, wants)? And, we purchase with such frequency that we are hard put to have the time to pay attention to the process.

The practice of love, in the deepest sense of its meaning, is one way to bring healing through the consummation of purchase transactions.

Closing

The primary purpose of this inquiry is to connect qualities of soul to the qualities of financial transactions. I am asking myself, and the reader, to take a deeper look at our economic life, to recognize that how we are with our transactions inwardly is just as important as how we conduct them outwardly. It is a step toward integrating espoused and practiced values through our finances, a step toward reawakening the sacredness of our economic life. In the passage from the *Four Quartets*, what T. S. Eliot is urging us to do is to set aside all assumptions, cultural conditioning, and expectations—whether about the future (hope), present (love), or past (faith)—and for each of us to live into what our soul has to tell us. When the soul inquiry we carry is about money and financial transactions, our place in them and their place in us, we may very well be on the frontier of transformative exploration: "So the darkness shall be the light, and the stillness the dancing." The practice of faith, hope, and love in financial transactions will then also invite that kind of transformation in others—as they experience the expression of inner values and are touched by their own.

PART III

A Wealth of Transformation

Interviews Exploring Money and Spirit

An Interview with Jacob Needleman

As part of RSF Social Finance's research process and growing collaboration of partners in transforming the way the world works with money, I have been honored to cross paths with some remarkable people who care deeply about understanding and inviting the presence of spirit in our evolving culture. One of those individuals is Jacob Needleman, who graciously agreed to this interview. As a professor of philosophy, Needleman has published and lectured on a broad range of topics, including money, philosophy, religion, and psychology. These have found expression in his books, such as *Why Can't We Be Good?*, *A Sense of the Cosmos: The Encounter of Modern Science and Ancient Truth*, *The Way of the Physician*, *Lost Christianity*, and, with John Piazza, *The Essential Marcus Aurelius*, to name a few. His book *Money and the Meaning of Life* is an extraordinary and engaging exploration of the historical and archetypal reality of money in our culture. In *The American Soul: Rediscovering the Wisdom of the Founders*, he explores the genealogy of the founding spirit of the United States. As is evident from this conversation, his insight and wisdom have the quality of inexhaustible wealth.

This interview was conducted in February 2004.

JB: What is America's particular mission in relation to money and economics?

JN: America's mission in relation to business goes back to the Enlightenment era, to the idea—which, in the light of modern history, may seem mere fantasy— that the money motive could be a force that could blunt some of the really violent and destructive passions of humankind. Enlightenment thinkers, such as Francis Hutcheson, David Hume, Adam Smith, and others, made a distinction between what could generally be termed the *passions* and the *interests*. The *passions* were those violent egoistic impulses that tended to result in physical and social destruction. The *interests* were often selfish certainly, but they had to do with stability, property, possessions, and bourgeois values. To put it simply: war and killing were very bad for business!

Although Enlightenment thinkers were certainly realistic about the flaws of human nature, they posited a theory that the money impulse, as reflected in the emerging system of capitalism, could become a moderating force in human life. Money-making was sometimes spoken of as a "calm passion." That was certainly an idealistic view of money, which formed part of the economic background in the founding and early development of capitalism in the United States.

Another comparable, but historically more efficacious idea, has to do with the play of forces affecting a culture (much in the way that forces operate in the Newtonian universe). This is our principle of the separation of powers in the United States government. You have a benign mutual interference of opposing forces that blunts any particular wolf-like aggrandizement or attack from one part of society on another part of society. Having three powers, the legislative, executive, and judicial, was a brilliant conceptual framework. It is the opposite of having a monarch, a single force that can do things very efficiently, including killing everybody.

Another idea was property. Jefferson and other people of that time wanted property to be the fundamental element in the country, rather than money. It was Alexander Hamilton who monetized America, who felt that the power of money as an instrument was the more important part.

Property is a very interesting and sophisticated concept. The interaction of mind and nature creates property. You have a mind that makes something happen—you do something, and then there is property. This view of individual ownership, of property, had to do with the support of individual development and well-being. Ownership of property could provide a base of material security necessary for the pursuit of more spiritual goals. And, of course, property ownership was understood to be an effective counterforce to the tendency of the state to assume too much authority and political control. These ideas are among the most important elements constituting America's mission and challenge around money.

Consider now the negative aspect of this mission, which has perhaps resulted in the power of money crowding out essential human values. Once the spiritual goal, or the moral or aesthetic element of life is diminished, then everything gets seen in terms of money. The means become the end and money becomes equated with wealth. But money is not wealth; money is a means for wealth, in the human sense of the term.

Money is a means, a necessary means, and a useful means. Money is a really brilliant piece of social technology. It enables people to share and exchange even in a very large community, and to recognize the reality of interdependence. So it is, and is meant to be, an instrument of community. Our aim should be to restore it to that noble function.

JB: So, if it's not wealth, what does money represent?

JN: What is money? It's nothing and it's everything at the same time. It's a social promise, a representation of work. It represents the desire part of human nature which is so strong. In one sense, money is nothing, and in another sense it's the bottom line. Money makes things real in human life. One has to acknowledge that money has this power. People tend not to want to see it that way, or else they give it too much power.

JB: Is that because they haven't worked on their own inner relationship to it?

JN: It's very hard for most of us. I don't know anybody who is normal about money. I don't even know what it would mean to be normal about money. You would not know how a person is about money until you're dealing with him or her. You and I are both filled with contradictions about money. I know I am. In this sense, money in our society is a golden key to self-knowledge. If you want to become aware of your contradictions, study how you think, feel, and behave in relation to money.

In my book *The American Soul*, I retell the story of America in the light of spiritual values. And I'm wondering about a new myth of America rooted in its actual history, but deeper than we now think of it. I've seen America as the protector, the guardian of the spiritual search. Its governmental structure can be understood as a great protector of human beings' freedom to come together in community to search for the conscience within. That's our ultimate freedom.

Otherwise, our freedom is childish. Freedom to shop—that's not why our forefathers fought and died! Their aim was something much more spiritual. The pursuit of happiness was not meant to be the pursuit of pleasure, but the pursuit of virtue. Virtue brings happiness. America is a place where people can come together and search for truth, for what is really human. That right is still protected, even in this post-9/11 era. America is the strongest physical force on the earth, militarily, culturally, and economically. Its strength is justified and will serve as long as it is protecting the conditions that support this spiritual need. If it ever loses this metaphysical mission, it will no longer be of any use, and probably the world won't want to keep it.

America is still the guardian of the spiritual search. That doesn't mean our president, governors, or senators know about this. Perhaps most of them don't care at all about such things. They don't have to, as long as they protect the structure that protects us. Really there are not very many places where you are quite as free as we are here, to speak, create associations, to protest.

JB: You're saying that the American government is structured to assure freedom. If freedom is a cultural value and practice, America's diversity presents unusual challenges for governance.

JN: America has to do with no ethnic identity, no cultural identity in that sense. It's an identity of the spirit, of the mind. It's an idea. It's a country based on great ideas, not on ethnicity, not on heredity. Granted it falls short, but still the structure is there to protect it.

Thomas Paine made a distinction in *Common Sense* between government and society. Government, he said, was tough, strong, and punitive, like armor and law; and society is softer and gentler. I would say society operates more in the realms of aesthetics and moral values. Government is legal; society is ethical. The purpose of government is to protect society. I've extrapolated that to—the heart of society is spiritual community. Government protects society, and the heart of society is the search for inner conscience, inner truth. It doesn't mean everybody out there has to have a spiritual search. What I mean is that human life is ultimately justified only in terms of the spiritual search. The metaphysical question is: Why are we on earth? What is a human being? What are we here for? We're an evolving entity. As Rudolf Steiner and all the great teachers have said, we are here to grow through a specific kind of inner struggle, to become what we are meant to be as the image of God. Perhaps not everyone has to be engaged in that way, but if some people are, then they are working for the whole of humanity.

JB: Is it natural irony that people deeply engaged in spiritual research frequently can't handle money?

JN: There is a misunderstanding of what the spiritual quest is. There are two parts of human nature, what the Jewish mystics call "the evil impulse" (the *yetzer ha ra*) and "the good impulse" (the *yetzer ha tov*). The evil impulse is not really evil in the ordinary sense; it is only evil when it is cut off from all relation to the good impulse and then usurps the whole of life. The function of the "evil" impulse is to engage outwardly and fully in life, to create, to do, to own, to have families, to write books, to accomplish things. The good impulse is to come toward the inner divine unity, to withdraw from the outward expansion of the self in order to be in touch with God. These are two parts of human nature that are described, often mythically and symbolically, in almost every great spiritual tradition. Our role is to harmonize these two within ourselves, and only then can we become what we are meant to be—fully human beings created in the image and likeness of God.

Each of us is living in a body, in a world of matter, which we are supposed to inhabit in an honorable human way to serve each other. Our relationship to God is only visible or even justifiable through serving each other. So, you have to honestly acknowledge the part of yourself that is worldly. Those who have trouble with money, not just spiritual people, but a lot of artistic types, are people who don't know how to deal with their worldly part.

Money in itself is not spiritual. But, the question of the place of money is a deeply spiritual question, because it means the place of that part of ourselves. Money is the part that organizes half of our life. If you don't take care of the outer part, the inner part will come to a halt, then you won't be fully human.

JB: If one really deals with the monetary realm, does that free up the capacity to work on oneself and in the culture?

JN: Not only freeing up capacity, but also giving oneself the space. If one uses that space just to make more money—that is foolish. If one uses that space just to get power, then the freedom that money has brought is violated.

JB: Conversely, though, I have heard it said, "Well, I've got my spiritual life in order, why isn't the money taking care of itself?"

JN: You can't have your spiritual life in order unless you take care of the worldly part too. Now we're all too familiar with the person who thinks the worldly part is the only part. That's of course a massive mistake. That's what America's problem is right now.

Up to a point the worldly part contradicts the spiritual part. That is what interests me. If I have to make a deal where you lose and I win, I say, "Oh well, that's the way money is, that's the way it works, that's okay. I'm not doing anything evil toward you." The pure spirit doesn't particularly want possessions. The pure spirit wants only to see, to contact God with love. But, man is not just a pure spirit. He's got the part that wants sex, money, power, appreciation, health. A fully developed man or woman harmonizes those two.

There is a kind of desire that is normal. We have a body. A body needs food, sex, water, comfort, warmth. The body really has desires which are part of our heredity. It's not just a survival thing. It's a human thing. But the desire nature can be inflamed or turned into craving, or egoistic fantasy, so that it becomes what we call obsessed—where the body's desires or social desires become the sole source of meaning. Then, desire becomes a problem and an illusion that one has to work to dispel, because one is trying to get from these desires something one can only get from a relationship with something higher in oneself. Desires are meant to serve a human being's life, but they're not the main aim in life.

JB: One could consider that we live in a currency of desires.

JN: That's what money serves as now. When the great spiritual traditions speak about the evil of desire, they're speaking of obsession, of craving. But it has been misinterpreted in a deadly way, so that all desires are seen as bad, and that becomes anti-life hypocrisy. So the honest recognition of the legitimacy of desire is an interesting part of spiritual life and part of the money issue, too.

However, the money game, which everyone needs to play, has entered into every part of our life now. The monetization of our society has become a very serious problem. Everything has a price tag. People of sensitivity know something's wrong with this.

Desire has become inflamed. All the great traditions say that the desire-nature left to itself just wants more and more. The body doesn't know about the spirit. It's an uneducated body, it just wants and wants. This desire-nature has been part of the human condition in all societies. The human fall is the desire-nature left to itself. It's wrapped up with the ego in that case, and the ego with the desire nature. Those two go together. They produce the fallen human being.

In the Tibetan tradition, there is a symbol of the hungry ghost. The hungry ghost is a being with a big belly and a tiny mouth, and the belly and the head and arms are really not quite connected. The more it eats, the more it wants. Anything it eats, burns as it goes down its throat. That's the inflamed desire-nature, and that's our society. We want and want, with advertising and social conditioning, to have more, new, better, and this is killing us all.

This is why we really need ideals back in our culture. How many shirts does a person need? How many houses do you really need? You need to have a gracious life, but how much do you need? And for young people it's terrible. Our young women and men are constantly seduced into wanting more and more, under the illusion that that will bring real happiness. And it doesn't.

I think the answer to consumerism is that people are starved for real ideas. The materialism of the American soul is a disease of the mind starved for ideas and ideals. Putting real ideas back into the culture will chip away at the force of materialism. The American founders had ideals about virtue, about soul, the human spirit, the mind, happiness. We have to bring those ideals back into the culture, as someone such as Steiner and others were and are trying to do. American values are good if they're deeply enough interpreted and understood. But the values our kids are being taught in school do not point to the soul, they point to something else. Social justice is fine, but unless it's pointing to the soul in some way, it's going to be just a refined version of materialism.

JB: Is there a contradiction between the bodily force of desire, and money, which is completely abstract with virtually no "body" at all? Does one just feed the other?

JN: You're right, it's gotten so abstract what money stands for, and yet at the same time it's very clear: for one dollar you buy such-and-such a thing. There's some kind of a mysterious contract, an agreement. It seems so unreal when you think about it, but so real when you deal with it. The poor guy on the street can't get a meal with abstract dollars.

JB: Is there ever alignment between what we spend our money on and our real values?

JN: In fact that disconnect happens a lot. For people who are not used to keeping a record of what they spend money on, it's a great exercise to do it for a week. What we spend money on also expresses what we value. It's an x-ray of our own contradictions; and we are full of contradictions, as is our culture. Money is the instrument of organizing one half of our nature, because meaning only comes from balancing the two parts. So money can buy you anything except meaning.

The first step to finding balance is to study our attitudes toward money. Our attitudes are full of hypocrisy. Most of us either value it too much or not enough. But it's really important to give one's attention to money and to examine one's assumptions about it. To do anything in this world, to help it, you need money. To really be good at the game of money and not be devoured by money is a great achievement. Ultimately, money, like every truly human creation, is meant to be an instrument of love, an instrument of service. That's what I think.

An Interview with an Anonymous Donor

To give anonymously is considered by some to be one of the highest forms of philanthropy, because it eliminates the expectation of recognition from the giving process. To speak of oneself anonymously, to speak with openness about one's inner path and processes, asks the reader to let go of the identity of the speaker and instead recognize the value of what is spoken. This interview is an inquiry into spirituality and philanthropy through the voice of an anonymous investor and donor. In the interview, the donor articulates the path, trials, and vision developed and practiced over many years. The donor has founded and advised not-for-profits and schools, has farmed and parented, and been a long-term supporter of new paradigm thinking, as will become evident in the interview. It was an honor to witness and record this conversation, to hear the humor and wisdom, and the devotion to spiritual practice as it informs profound philanthropic and humanitarian work in the world.

This interview was conducted in February 2002.

JB: In light of your meditative practice and path, what is your relationship to money?

AD: I think it's an important question. My relationship to money is not necessarily your average one. Nor is its relationship to me. That's another story. I come from a business family and my background is Jewish. Because of this particular background, money is not in the shadow as much as it is in the broader society of America. I've been involved with non-profits for many years, and not in the business world. However, I have an unusual attitude about money, more matter-of-fact.

JB: Can you go back into how that matter-of-factness came about? Does it affect the way you do philanthropy?

AD: These views are imparted through an inception process more than through what is said. Those of us who are parents are horrified by what our kids have soaked up from us without our intending it at all. Knowledge and values are transferred by osmosis to the benefit or detriment of everyone. I could tell you I learned about money through dinner table conversations, or going to the office with my dad on Saturday, and overhearing him on the telephone, or listening when his brothers would come over. The women would be talking about hair salons and their nails, which I found boring after 30 seconds. I tended to listen to the men talking about what had been going on with the business. They would tell stories of things they'd experienced. I just soaked up a certain point of view.

JB: Then you were following a natural interest.

AD: To tell you the truth, I was anything but interested in doing philanthropy. I'm getting interested now, but it's not something that I found instantly as my calling. I wanted to be a psychotherapist. I wanted to do farming and mothering. I knew that that was my piece to do in the world, and what I wanted to be involved with. I didn't feel at all that way about philanthropy. I actually didn't have the opportunity to be philanthropic until I was in my thirties. Even now, I don't do philanthropy on a full-time basis. I spend as little time as possible on it because it interferes with my vocation and personal life.

On the other hand, the world is in desperate need. For karmic reasons, I seem to be in a position to be able to direct significant resources toward helping things that need to happen in order for us to gracefully move to the next stage of our evolution on this earth with as little suffering as possible. I can't *not* help with that, given the position I'm in. It's really out of a sense of responsibility that I come to philanthropy.

JB: Would you link that sense of responsibility with your spiritual practice?

AD: I link it to my spiritual self. I almost hesitate to use the word spiritual. I would say that in the deepest part of myself, capital S, or mind in the greater sense, that lives on even past the body. That part of me has its roots in a common source of all being. *Bodhicitta* is the word used to describe this. In the language of my lineage it means enlightened mind. It's from that that we can feel another's suffering and the urge to alleviate it. That is why I do philanthropy.

JB: That is a very beautiful and inspiring image. Can you speak about your spiritual practice?

AD: Every day I start with a meditation. I use this practice to get the bracken away, and to get as close to the essence as I can. This essence is actually how the Tibetans describe what we call enlightenment. There's a word for Buddha in Tibetan that is not the same as it is in Sanskrit. In Sanskrit, Buddha means awakened one. In my lineage it means cleansed one. We believe that one cleanses away mistaken views. This makes it possible to experience reality directly. I feel I'm in a process of doing that. I find when I'm more conscious of this process, things go better, not only in philanthropy but also in anything I do, whether it's mothering or driving down the street. I'm conducting my life more consciously. I've learned this lesson the hard way. I have learned the value and effectiveness of meditation, prayer, and other practices. Without it, I have suffered, gotten off track, and wasted a lot of time.

I started meditation as a daily practice when I was about twenty. I didn't have instruction, so I wasn't very good at it. I happen to have a naturally active mind, so I didn't have a natural talent for quieting my mind. It was a struggle. Even though I wasn't doing very well, when I stopped, things went badly. I could feel that I wasn't pursuing my life as right on target as I had been in the past.

I decided when I resumed meditation practices, that I would need instruction. I came upon a Tibetan lama, at the time. I didn't really care which flavor it was as long as the teacher was somebody I could really connect well with and who really was accomplished. I have been studying with him for about seven years. I always felt that pursuing a spiritual path was an important part of my life. When I found a teacher my practice became a more vital part of my life.

Enlightenment is a central goal. Actually, that's what we're always pursuing, waking, sleeping, chewing on our problems, all the time in life. The question is, how consciously are we going directly toward that?

JB: Why did you want to be a psychotherapist?

AD: You want the full analysis? I don't know fully why. I've always been fascinated by how the mind works. I've been a people watcher since I was little. Another piece is that it feels good to alleviate suffering. And, I think I'm a born teacher. When somebody comes to me with their life in a knot, they need a fellow human being to help them look at it, figure out which strings to pull, and how to loosen the knot a little bit. I love to help with that process. I see myself as an ally in their inquiry into their own mind. Another aspect is that I enjoy just the experience of connecting with people on a deep level.

JB: You mentioned the notion that money is kind of a shadow issue. What did you mean by that?

AD: One has to look to the roots of our culture. The church people weren't supposed to handle money—a ridiculous notion because the Roman Empire was being run through the church. They had a lot of power, and yet the cardinals and bishops weren't supposed to be handling money because it would dirty their hands. This attitude was certainly deeply ingrained within the Christian world. Until relatively recently from a historical perspective, not very many people had or earned money. Those who weren't land holders or rulers were either farmers or church people. From the perspective of my culture, once the Jews were forbidden to own land and were periodically being driven from it, they were newcomers wherever they went. What could they do? They had to be professionals. All through the countries of the Diaspora they spoke a common language, which meant they could do commerce in a way that others couldn't. They were both pushed into it and drawn into it by the particular event of the Diaspora.

Doing business is something that my family has probably been engaging in for a couple of millennia. We had to be really good at it or we were not going to eat. My family usually lived in a town near Kiev in Russia. They would also go back and forth between there and Kiev, where they had the opportunity to make more money. There was a government quota for Jews allowed to come into Kiev and live there on a temporary basis, even if it was for three years. Some Jews were selected because they were needed for a particular function. Once that function was fulfilled, the Jews were thrown out until they were needed again. My family would go home, then return to Kiev for a while. This is as I understand it. Because we were better at grain trade, we were often the ones asked to come and go into Kiev, which then allowed us more opportunity. We've had an immigrant mentality for a couple thousand years. We'd have to perform better than everybody else just in order to make it. We feel our life depends on accomplishing whatever it is, and doing it really well.

JB: In all that shift of commerce there is trading of money and goods. Though Jews were not allowed to own land, they could still accumulate a surplus of money or wealth. Accumulation tends to bring power and authority. Is this notion applicable?

AD: We couldn't own land. We could own things, and consequently we exercised influence. The quality of commerce was itself affected. I have thought about this in relation to current non-profit and for-profit activities. If I really want to affect change in society, it seems to me the for-profit sector is what really is affecting people's lives on a more vast and basic scale than non-profits. When something hits the for-profit world, societal change happens. The non-profit world can plant seeds and hopefully begin movement in a certain direction. At first it's probably not very profitable. For the change to really happen, it's got to go into the for-profit sector.

JB: But that change has not necessarily been for the better.

AD: We see the power exercised by what they thought was profitable. Commerce is driving things in our society. In past societies, almost any of them, the religious institutions were also promoting culture. Michelangelo was mostly supported by the church and the Medici family as patrons. William Irwin Thompson, an historian, in looking at the history of humanity and change, said that the spiritual visionaries were the first ones to get the new pattern. The artists were next. They had the ability then to communicate it further, and, thus, have a very important function in society as far as changing paradigms. Then came the business people. Of course, bringing up the rear were the political leaders. We're in a moment in history right now, when there's a paradigm shift that's trying to happen.

JB: Can you name or articulate the paradigm shift?

AD: Look at this on a continuum of humanity's evolution to make sense of this moment of paradigm shift. Humanity's evolution parallels the maturation process of a human being. Individual human beings start out being one with the mother in the womb. After they're born, they're still attached to the mother through the breast. First they take little steps away, start showing ego development, and then they start saying "no," which is establishing their own will. They also develop the conscious mind more. These I think of as more masculine qualities—the conscious will and the ego. Whereas, the mother and unconscious are more feminine things. By teenagerhood, they know much better than both parents. Significant individualizing has taken place, and they tend to believe only in themselves. The ego is really out there. That's what they're about. They've got to be so full of themselves that they're willing to withstand the rigors of the outside world and leaving home. At some point they go through a prodigal son experience through which they realize, "Gosh, maybe I don't know everything." Mark Twain said something like: "When I was in my teens my father just didn't know a thing. But by my early twenties it was amazing how much the man had learned."

We went through a process in which the pendulum swung from matriarchy to patriarchy, from the feminine to the masculine. In an individual it then begins to move towards center again out of the natural seeking for balance. Humanity is now at that point. We've developed the conscious mind, the ego, scientific process, and know more than father spirit and mother earth. Being quite full of ourselves, we've come to the point where we are starting to realize that we need to work on these greater things, to bring more balance. Hence, there is the emerging importance of the feminine, and the receding of the masculine.

Intuition is valued in business more now than in the past, as are relationships, process, and group facilitation. Corporations have a need for these values and qualities. This is where we are in the paradigm shift.

Another aspect of the paradigm change is that the understanding of power begins to shift so that it is no longer power-*over*. Currently this is about the only form of power that is acknowledged. Power-*with* and power-*within* are feminine forms of power. Power-*within* is something that America hasn't acknowledged at all. However, going within is something I've been doing a lot. I have found it a great source of power because it connects with the enlightened mind.

JB: We may be driven to a paradigm shift simply by survival.

AD: Allow me a kind of image or metaphor. We've been standing on this piece of ground, an island in the ocean, if you will. Land masses come up and go down. This one has been here for a long time. Now it is old and crumbling. People tend to be conservative by nature. Consequently, they say, "Oh, it's crumbling. We just have to use more and more resources to patch it together." Well, of course it's all crumbing, because it's just finished. At a certain point, it will be all patches and there will be no substance of the original thing left. Meanwhile, there is another land mass that's coming up, just naturally emerging.

In the spring, asparagus comes up anew. We cut it and cut it, yet it keeps coming in great big fat sprouts that want to turn into these beautiful ferns that tower over our heads. There is an extraordinary amount of upward growing energy in those tips of asparagus. Like the asparagus, the tip of the rising land mass has a lot of cohesiveness, strength, and upward energy in it. The other land mass has crumbling downward energy. Those of us who are able to see the rising land mass, and know that that's the place to go, need to build a bridge from the old crumbling one to the new emerging one.

JB: How would you know a new paradigm institution or organization? Is it intuition? Are there some criteria?

AD: You could say that the criteria support your intuitive knowing. One characteristic is whether it practices power-*with* or power-*over*? A second is, does it take the context of the global picture into account? I also want to know the people, how they are working together, their system. If it's not a healthy system, it can be the greatest idea in the world, but nothing will come of it. These are some ways that I can tell. Of course, one's sense of intuition is critical. I identify myself as being part of that growing network of people who have a sense of this emerging land mass and who want to build a bridge to it. I consider RSF an important part of that network.

If I'm going to put my own personal energy and money towards something, one thing that will happen, first of all, is that I experience an intuitive, energized "yes." The second thing that I experience is that I cannot *not* do it. In reality, we know right action in and through our hearts.

An Interview with Charles Terry

This interview with Charles Terry offers a rare insight into the world of philanthropy and money from the perspective of a former foundation officer, attorney, and social service advocate. His deep wisdom and experience radiate through his insights into the personal integration of accomplishing social change through vocation with the cultivation of inner life and spiritual practice.

Charles is currently president of Terry-MacGregor Associates, philanthropic and nonprofit/NGO advisors. He was formerly the director of philanthropy at the Rockefeller Family Office in New York City, and president of The Philanthropic Collaborative, a public charity. Following graduation from Harvard Law School and a stint in corporate law, he chose to work for minimal wages in practicing urban, community, and poverty law in New York City. For eight years he was a professor of law at New York University School of Law, where he founded and directed the Urban Law Clinical Program. Before joining the Rockefeller family, Charles was vice president of the International Center for Integrative Studies, and served as an ICIS delegate to the United Nations. As a part of his work with ICIS, he helped to found and served for 10 years as the executive director of The Door—A Center of Alternatives, an internationally recognized multi-service health, education and arts center for youth in New York City. Through his work there Charles began his deep engagement with and learned about, philanthropy, money, and the foundation world.

Charles and his wife Betsy MacGregor are working in Africa, in collaboration with organizations such as Ashoka and Partnership for Youth Empowerment–Global, to help alleviate poverty and enhance opportunities for the many emerging young leaders and social entrepreneurs who are leading a re-awakening of Africa, and promoting greater connection and cooperation between Africa and the western world.

This interview was conducted in March 2003.

JB: Your involvement in philanthropy began out of volunteer service and the recognition of a social need. Were you out fundraising in the foundation milieu on behalf of The Door?

CT: As The Door's program grew I got involved in raising money for it, because it became clear that we could serve a lot more kids with more money, staff, and space. First, we received federal government funding. Then as our needs continued to grow, we began to look to the private sector. We went to foundations and individual philanthropists. This required quite a different approach than reading regulations and writing grants. Building relationships was really important, even for government funding.

I eventually took a leave of absence from teaching to be the Executive Director at The Door for a period of time. I began to meet with foundations, corporate executives and private philanthropists. The Door was such a fabulous place—people would come down to visit and they experienced the energy of the kids and the creativity of the programs—it was an easy sell if you could get people there. That was my first contact with the world of philanthropy. But, we never had enough money. It was very frustrating to me to think that in such a wealthy city (New York) it was such a struggle to raise the resources to provide free services to these kids who were so beautiful—they have huge problems, but given support and opportunities they are so creative and talented.

JB: Do you think there was some value in that struggle? Maybe there was some positive dynamic that came as consequence of it.

CT: I ask myself that question a lot. Also I asked myself, "If we were comfortable financially what would that mean?" Part of me really wanted that and felt we deserved it. At the same time I felt being on the edge was very helpful and that it was the right place to be. There is so much need that there never will be enough money until our whole concept of money and how we use it changes. There is always tension between what you can do and how much money you have. It was a challenge having to raise all this money all the time and keep up relationships, but there is some natural value in that process. One of the reasons I'm particularly interested in money and finance is that one of the last things I did with The Door was to help them find a new home after its 14-year lease ran out. We had the "crazy" idea of trying to buy a building. We started by getting banks, foundations and others involved in one way or another. It became an $18 million project leveraged with foundation PRI's [program related investments] and grants, bank loans and a tax-exempt bond issue. We bought and converted a building in Soho (NYC) into a nonprofit condominium that's still operating today. It is an example of the magic around money, since we accomplished an $18 million new facility project having started with zero money or assets.

After that point, I decided to take a self-created sabbatical. I went to Asia for three months, and finally spent a few weeks in Nepal up in the mountains. One of the things that came to me was the idea of philanthropy. Something about money had always interested me ever since I first chose not to go the path of making lots of money through practicing law. The experience with the capital building project for The Door really intrigued me because of the relationships that were possible with funders, philanthropists and investors.

When I came home, a good friend of mine said, "By the way the Rockefeller family is looking for a Director of Philanthropy," and would I be interested. He kept encouraging me, so I agreed to meet with them. The first meeting I had with the family was with Steven Rockefeller who is one of Nelson Rockefeller's sons and a very special person. He was head of the family philanthropy committee at that time. I was so moved and touched by his deep values, his caring about the world, his commitment and his own spirituality, that it stepped up my level of interest. That led to a series of meetings with lots of family members and committees.

They offered me the job of director of philanthropy. By then I had decided that this was a place where I felt I could make a difference in the world. Interestingly, Kitty Telsch, *New York Times*'s writer on philanthropy at that time, wrote a story about my appointment with a headline like: "Rockefeller Family Hires Idealist as Head of Philanthropy." She quoted me asking something like, "Is it possible to make a difference to the streets of New York and the world from the 56th floor of Rockefeller Center?" That was a real dilemma for me.

JB: Did you experience the issues that accompany the typical assumptions, even projections, around power and wealth?

CT: It certainly brought me into the issue of the separation among people of wealth, people that don't have money, and service providers who run programs. But, it didn't feel like a separation based on power; although it's clear that power is a major issue. I felt more the gap of understanding, communication, and connection.

My direct work was with Rockefeller family members personally, their personal giving and their private foundations, with a fairly large group of fourth- and fifth-generation members. The Rockefeller Family Office decided to expand its services with the result that I worked with a number of other wealthy families who were starting or expanding foundations. Many were also in intergenerational transition from a founding generation to the next generation. This next generation sometimes had a major increase or decrease in assets, and family issues frequently had to be resolved. The questions and issues were: how you cope with these issues, how you give money away meaningfully, how you meet the differing needs of family members and still find a common purpose.

I was also President of the Philanthropic Collaborative (TPC), which had just been created as I was coming in. The Philanthropic Collaborative is a public charity that has donor advised funds, special project funds, and collaborative funds, and was created to facilitate philanthropy and help Rockefeller family members and other donors collaborate on projects. Some wonderful collaborations were created such as the Northern Forests Land Collaboration, which has helped to preserve 26 million acres of forests in Northern New England and New York. Another major use of TPC was for people who didn't want to create a foundation to create a donor advised fund; many were created and used to enhance and focus the donor's giving.

JB: How would you characterize philanthropy?

CT: When I'm invited to speak, I like to talk about philanthropy as "love of humanity." That is the root of the word and the heart of the concept. My approach to donors, especially new ones, is to help them get in touch with their caring about humanity, society or their local community, and to base their philanthropy on that deep caring.

JB: Is the working assumption here that philanthropy is primarily about money?

CT: In some ways I challenge that assumption about the philanthropy. Although the common definition is the giving of money—and this is important—I believe philanthropy incorporates other kinds of giving, including giving of yourself, your time and skills, and other non-monetary resources. These are very important. Yet, at the same time, there are huge and critical issues about money in our world.

JB: Can you say more about what the issue is with money? Is it just too much in too few places, and not enough where it is really needed?

CT: There are many ways to talk about money. Money is like a natural resource that should or could be available for the whole planet. Like air or water, it's something that can help if necessary to sustain the planet and its inhabitants. There are vast accumulations of money that, if put to use for the common good with the collective wisdom we have, could transform this planet into quite a wonderful place. It's of course more complicated than that, but with the right consciousness, money could be used in a very positive way on behalf of the whole planet, towards a world that works for everybody. That's one thought I have about money—that the accumulated wealth could be used in a very constructive and healing way.

JB: Why do you think it's accumulated to the extent that it has?

CT: Releasing accumulations of money would be good not just for the world, but also for those who are holding it. There's a tremendous potential for wellness and healing through conscious use and release of money by wealth holders and society overall. This gets us to why money is hoarded. It's complex, but the first word that comes to mind is "fear." Having money is an illusory way of thinking and feeling you're more secure. It also has to do with the idea that my value as a person relates to how much money I have. Again, this is illusory, but that's how it plays out in the public culture.

JB: Can you say more about money as a natural resource, because one doesn't usually think about it in that way. To my mind money is more human artifice, an invention of human consciousness.

CT: Money is certainly a resource. It ought to be a common resource rather than something that's owned by relatively few people. But I want to take this a little further. There is something in what human beings are and do that converts material in nature into money. It may be taking minerals out of the ground; it may be the labor of people that goes into creating goods or services. Money is like human and earth energy condensed into a new kind of matter. There's spiritual energy in there, too, which I don't fully understand. Where do these forms of energy come from? A good part of it comes from the sun, the earth and humanity. Money is a way of concretizing and storing that energy. In that sense it is a natural phenomenon.

One of the things that I learned, in working with the Rockefellers, for example, is that money is very powerful. One sees a building going up next door, and money is making that happen. Whether you like it or not is a different story. But money has a powerful energy. To the degree we use our consciousness, our spiritual awareness, in using that energy, it can have quite positive transformative effects. One has to remain aware, of course, that it can also be destructive.

JB: Isn't there a difference if one relates to one's wealth as power rather than as responsibility?

CT: One way I think about money is that its energy is neutral. A key is how it is used. Another key is the person who's holding it: how they're holding it, what their motivation is, their consciousness and values. I think it can be held as a resource for the benefit of the whole in a kind of public trust. Such a person could say, "Okay, I have been fortunate enough to either inherit or earn all this money, but I know the nature of money is such that I hold it for the greater good"—that's one way of holding it. Another factor is the level of awareness and maturity of the person holding the money. Based in part on the values of our culture, for example, you can hold it and say, "with this money comes responsibility." This is actually one of the core values of the Rockefeller family—that with wealth comes responsibility. What is the scope of that responsibility vis-à-vis the public good? Does that mean only the interest earned on the wealth is a public trust, or does it mean the whole corpus? These are significant questions which some wealth holders are exploring.

JB: The fundamental distinction you make between owning money and serving as a trustee for it is an important one. Isn't our culture mostly in the ownership mode?

CT: There is a parallel between water and money here. I see money as similar to water, as a natural resource that flows and doesn't necessarily belong to anybody but it exists to serve everyone. What's fascinating is that we're beginning to subject water to commercial ownership and control. It's deeply troubling. It is one of my hopes to release money to flow more freely into our society, into those places where it's needed, to let it flow in the way it might naturally flow without private interests damming it up. Why should we be able to hoard money? I understand that there have been times in history when it was illegal to earn interest on money—or even that money lost value (negative interest) if it wasn't used or circulated. Think about how different our world would be under this system.

JB: You are touching on some ethical and moral issues around money.

CT: The issue is *on whose behalf* is the money held. It raises some very basic human and values issues. It goes to respect for others and their well being, and how much we are truly a community, a human family, both locally and globally. Do we really see ourselves in some way as brothers and sisters? As related? Is it fine for me to have all this money but for you to be starving to death? Is that OK?

JB: Are you pointing to a disconnection between ethics, morality, and money—and what more the technology and sophisticated uses of money could make possible?

CT: Philanthropy is one of those areas that bridges from an older amoral view of money to an emerging view of money, which sees a greater connection with the common good. I've seen so often that philanthropy is transformative for the wealth holder. Often you see that people who hoard appear constricted and fearful and not very happy, but when they begin to give, even if it's not huge amounts, the act of giving is transformative and releasing for them. Psychological and spiritual evolution goes with the releasing of money, and philanthropy is one of the ways to do that. I see philanthropy as a great good in our culture. Some people would argue with that.

JB: What would the argument be?

CT: If we didn't have philanthropy, the problems would be more obvious. Philanthropy is a kind of a band-aid that allows our government and others to say that the poor are being taken care of. I can see some validity to this argument. Maybe things would get worse without philanthropy, and then, either they'd just keep getting worse, or we'd say, "We can't let this happen."

JB: I have a hard time with the band-aid viewpoint since it ignores the causes of the problems in the first place.

CT: I actually do, too. I can understand it as an argument, and I can see all the issues—the shadow side—around how we do philanthropy: that it is too controlling, not done strategically, separates the donor and the recipient. In general, however, as an element in our culture, philanthropy is a very good bridge for the giver and can help in terms of dealing with problems. It's in the direction of a different perspective on money. If we as a whole society, and the wealth holders in particular, changed the culture from hoarding to more giving, it would transform us—not only because of what the money would do, but because of what it would do for the culture that hoards and teaches hoarding. There's a benefit from a change in attitude, activity and consciousness around money, which as I understand it, is the purpose of the RSF Social Finance.

Morality can become something *external* that says I should give away money. My objective is *internal*—how do we get to the place inside us where we either don't need to hoard because we're not afraid and we trust life, and when we care enough about those others that we really want to give.

How we see and use money in our society is an expression of who we are. In that sense, it's the barometer. But I think the "who we are" is a product of history, culture and values. This country was created for certain reasons. Individualism was an important part of it. But, perhaps we have gone too far with the emphasis on and importance of the individual. This supports the justification for the entrepreneur—who is both a necessary part of and a gift to the society—to keep going and going and keeping and keeping. Another, more mature human expression is one that recognizes itself as part of the whole, as part of the community. My sense is that we as a society are very slowly moving to a more conscious, mature place which would give full freedom of expression to the individual as well as full respect for the other and the collective. This is a slow and painful process, and what we do with money is an expression of where we are in that process. Right now it's an expression of a fairly immature consciousness, like an adolescent who is so rambunctious and has huge amounts of energy but doesn't necessarily have clarity about what to do with it.

The self-serving use of money, as opposed to what you called full-service to society, is like an expression of where we are evolutionarily as a culture. What's needed is the kind of leadership that the RSF is providing, to begin to show the way to another approach to money. As people wake up they will notice that this actually serves them better than the old way, because hoarding or just making more and more money hasn't made them happy. I believe we are moving in this direction.

The more we can enter into stillness and quiet instead of the usual frenetic pace, the more we reflect on life and action—as individuals, as groups, and in society—the more we are likely to get some clarity around these issues of money. Money is now mostly electronic—it is barely physical at all and it is moving rapidly in cyberspace. While it is moving so fast one can hardly grasp it; but such movement also makes the possibility for change greater. Money is light—it is in the realm of spirit, of energy. What is money when you think about it on that level? Perhaps its very lightness foretells its transformation.

The individual journey toward greater awareness and wholeness has to go hand in hand with how one works with money. Fostering and supporting that journey is an important and vitally needed service that will encourage the healthy flow of money as a resource and be transformative for society.

An Interview with Krystyna Jurzykowski

This interview with Krystyna Jurzykowski speaks to the topic of spirit and philanthropy. Krystyna is one of the pioneers of the new heart-centered philanthropy. As you will see through the interview, her biography and life passions brought her to a relationship with nature that has both served the world of wildlife conservation and informed her of the inner landscape of her own nature. Her willingness and ability to reflect candidly on the connections between personal values and money are extraordinary. This inner journey has also led her to guiding spirit-based retreats and inquiries into destiny paths at her center called High Hope, adjacent to Fossil Rim Wildlife Center in Texas.

Krystyna was president, chair of the board, and co-owner of Fossil Rim Wildlife Center, one of the most unusual and widely-respected wildlife conservation and education centers in the world. She is an author on the topics of animals and nature, and serves as advisor and consultant to organizations and foundations including the Marion Institute, Big Mind, Beyond Boundaries, Animal Ambassadors, Equus Projects, Pleroma, and RSF's AnJel Fund.

This interview was conducted in August 2000.

JB: Since you have made a transition from Fossil Rim, perhaps you could reflect on how it came about in the first place.

KJ: The short story of how I got involved with Fossil Rim Wildlife Center resides in three words: *passion* around nature and animals, *ignorance* about the subject, and *destiny*. The journey has taught me that when one sets an intention through a clear question, it taps into what one's destiny is framed to be. Then all the forces work together to bring one toward that end.

Both my partner and I "retired" from business in 1983. Out of conversations about our life passions, a number of events occurred over the next two years. While we were living in Europe we saw a documentary on a British man named John Aspinal, who started several wildlife preserves. We were inspired by the difference he had made, so we started researching the underlying issues within wildlife conservation and habitat protection. This led us to Fossil Rim and eventually resulted in our saving what had once been a private wildlife ranch.

We got involved and quickly came to realize that the place was in crisis. Then we were named in a lawsuit, and we were forced to come to Texas to deal with the problem. I was resistant; we had no interest in moving back to the United States. The first few years were really tough; the word that kept coming to me was *commitment*. The larger forces at work compelled me to align myself with my values, my passion, and my money. And Texas did it. By 1988, we were living there full time. I'm a firm believer that our so-called "difficult experiences" really shape us. I've had a few key ones in my life. It's the grand paradox that when we lose, we actually gain.

Fossil Rim is beautiful—close to 3000 acres—in the northern highlands of what's called the hill country of Texas. The land is shaped like a hand. The fingers are thickly forested rims of oak and juniper forests, and between them are gently rolling and open grassland savannahs, very similar to landscapes in Africa like the Rift Valley in Kenya. In the United States, we are the closest thing to an African wildlife preserve. There are herds of African antelope, rhinos, and giraffes and other animals that roam different areas, 1100 animals in all. A staff of sixty-plus volunteers and interns are deeply involved in the work.

Our ultimate goal is to reintroduce these animals back into the wild, which leads us into dealing with human geo-political issues. Most of our work is with critically endangered species that have lost or are losing their habitat from human pressures. To be truly successful, wildlife conservation strategies have to include people, land and animals. One cannot discuss the health of animals without talking about the health of the land base and the people, be it in a village or city.

Fossil Rim is home to a diverse mix of programs and partnerships with conservation and wildlife organizations both in the United States and around the world. When we first became active, we knew so little about the conservation world, but we had a passion. We brought in a vice president from World Wildlife

Fund and started a non-profit to be in partnership with the existing sole proprietorship. But we found across the conservation world that very little money was being generated other than through government programs and philanthropy. We also became aware of the underlying assumptions that 501(c)(3)s and social organizations do "good" and the private sector corporations are "bad." We knew that this had to change. We felt that whatever the context, each person has to take responsibility for producing a change that has a positive impact on all dimensions of the socio-economic sectors. We also had a principle that whatever we did had to be replicable in the animals' countries of origin where we worked, and philanthropy didn't exist yet on a continent like Africa.

We started applying both philanthropic and entrepreneurial approaches to wildlife conservation. By the late 1980s we did a very controversial thing. We dissolved the 501(c)(3) and instead formed a privately held corporation, an investment vehicle to foster businesses that would in turn generate revenues to support the "philanthropic" aspects of our conservation efforts, be they education, research, training, endangered species breeding, and so forth. That was pretty radical at the time.

JB: Was there concern about Fossil Rim's dependence on you and your partners' investments to make it feasible?

KJ: At first, we were simply building capacity. Over time it became evident that the long-term health of the place had to be addressed. I started thinking about it on a deeper level. Any company or organization associated with one leader or funder is essentially a monoculture, and we know that is unsustainable. We engaged in a process to design a transition strategy that resulted in a fair and reasonable exit for the investors, changing Fossil Rim from a private ownership to a public non-profit with community-based board governance. The goal was to ensure a mission-related revenue stream and protect the land through conservation easements.

JB: You mentioned, aside from your passion and destiny path, that it was also your investment that made Fossil Rim happen. Do you see that as philanthropic work?

KJ: Absolutely, it's engaged, spirit-driven philanthropy.

JB: What do you mean by engaged philanthropy?

KJ: Hands-on. One can be philanthropic with one's time or resources, be they financial or other. I grew up in a home that was actively philanthropic. My father died when I was 14, and my mother died four years later. Very early on I was left an inheritance without much mentoring or directed education other than my own experiences and memories as a child. After my father's death, I experienced how money could corrupt and turn friendship into greed. At 18, I didn't want anything to do with it, so I denied my inheritance and went into business.

It wasn't until my 30s that I realized that I had certain passions within me that could be leveraged, acted upon, kindled, or rekindled, using my wealth as a resource. I really have to thank Jim, who's now my ex-husband and still my dear friend and partner at Fossil Rim, for helping me through that journey. He helped me look at money not as a curse or a guilt trip, but as energy, as a tool. In the 80s, I started actively looking at my wealth and becoming involved with several organizations. Today, my involvement with the organizations I financially support is either as a creative participant and advisor, or as a board member.

To develop Fossil Rim and support several other organizations, I blew all the rules held in the current conventional economic system by using about 85% of the corpus of my inheritance. In doing so I've had to push out the borders of acceptability in wealth generation and accumulation. I've often felt alone, though I knew I was really following my intuition.

JB: What were the other forces that were keeping you on your path, even though you were experiencing some exposure and vulnerability?

KJ: The word *commitment* comes up for me again. Fossil Rim has taught me the depth and unconditionality of real commitment. Above all else it has reconnected me to nature, and therefore essentially connected me to my own nature.

Growing up in Brazil as a young child I had the great fortune of living next to a jungle. The animals, the trees, all the beings of that environment were my first pals. When we moved out of Brazil and eventually to New York City—from one jungle to another—I buried my love of nature. I avoided my grief by becoming a city girl. Fossil Rim has helped me remember that we all have an incredible gift to be in communication and connected with all other beings, visible and invisible. I believe that we lose that ability as we get acculturated. For me it has been a process of re-membering myself within a larger community of life.

JB: Have you found colleagues on the cutting edge of philanthropy? Has there been a significant cultural shift in approaching or practicing philanthropy?

KJ: I've met a lot of people who have engaged in their own way, by beginning projects, starting their own foundations, or participating in the governance of organizations. However, there is something in the air now, especially in the last few years. This "something" is the realization that there is no difference between being of service to others and being of service to our own evolutionary awareness.

In the last year and a half, I have participated with a number of organizations and individuals who are questioning the whole world of philanthropy. They are applying rigorous inquiry into the hidden beliefs and underlying power dynamics within this culture. Just as many of us are looking at the educational, social, or economic systems and asking how they can work for everyone, we're also on the rim of an archaeological exploration of philanthropy. We are trying to understand the successes, failures, and where the borders themselves have to expand. A new language is needed. The word "philanthropy" itself— what does this imply? Many individuals and institutions, such as RSF, Marion and Fetzer Foundations among others, are all sensing that something more is needed. We've got to be more in relationship with ourselves and our projects, and work in alliance with like-minded individuals and organizations. It's about connection. How do we deepen our abilities to listen to what is emerging, and be willing to make the changes in ourselves?

I'm on the board of Marion Institute in Marion, Massachusetts. In March of last year, we had a meeting to examine the dynamics of giving and receiving, both in a philanthropic context and in our daily lives. Mark Finser was invited to this meeting because of RSF's groundbreaking efforts in the realm of

Donor Advised Funds, spirit and philanthropy. Innovative Frontiers, a Marion Institute initiative, was formed to create collaborative relationships as project partnerships between donors and grantees. Within this relationship is the inherent understanding that there is an exchange and flow of giving and receiving on many different levels. We must remember that financial resources are only one of many levels of exchange. It's a learning process, a way to pay attention to all the elements, behavior patterns, and belief systems that have built the building of philanthropy.

JB: Historically, philanthropists have not often spoken personally about their philanthropy, certainly not on the destiny level which you have addressed.

KJ: There is now much more dialogue and internal exploration into the meaning and use of money. How we make decisions of where and what to buy is in effect a philanthropic act. How I choose to use my time determines whether I am philanthropic with my inner self or not. Having just come out of a period of time where I was a classic workaholic, I'm seeing that I was actually quite miserly with time. Now I'm looking for much more balance.

We also have to look at the generation of capital. How is philanthropic capital generated? Are we being philanthropic and wise with our investments? We have to embrace both the light and shadow sides of this capital. We've got to seek meaning not only in the success of individual programs and initiatives we fund or invest in, but also in the larger perspective of *how* we do what we do. Are we connected, aware, and spiritually conscious?

JB: You have connected your spiritual philosophy with your understanding of money. That level of integration of values and money is unusual.

KJ: Money is a very wise teacher. I've been referred to as an artist and philosopher. I actually like to ask questions which have both inner and external applications. I have to live the research of those questions through my own experience.

JB: Would you say that money is a neutral but active reflector of one's self and values?

KJ: Yes, indeed—which is why I resonated immediately with RSF in spirit matters and money. Economics, family, community and spiritual life, are all simply contexts for us to become more aware of ourselves, and, therefore, more aware of others—to be of service to the totality of consciousness, not just our own quality of life.

JB: Since you are transitioning away from day-to-day work at Fossil Rim, what is next for you?

KJ: The stewardship at the heart of the place has been transferred in a good way. It's incredible to find this after many years of responsibility. I am creating space in my life. I'm still active and more of a nomad, not only in my private life, but also in being able to travel among different organizations. Just as the friendship has developed between me and RSF, I find myself helping to create connections between allies—making links for a purpose. Fossil Rim is my active philanthropic portfolio. To what degree do we initiate our own philanthropic portfolios in our lives—whether it's time, financial resources, sharing our networks, or helping to create webs of alliances so that individuals or institutions don't have to reinvent the wheel over and over? It's all about working in collaboration and cooperation rather than creating sovereign states of activity.

JB: You have an important message for people who are trying to find a good relationship to their money. The notion of engaged philanthropy is about how your heart guides your money and your actions. Understanding the constructive potential of this relationship is one of the important issues of our time.

KJ: Another important question from a cultural perspective is one of accumulation. For the twenty-first century, we have to ask the question of how much is enough. How much do we each really need? How do we make every decision of our lives as a meaningful part of a larger purpose? Money has created boundaries in our culture. How do we begin to learn that what is good for me has to be good for others, or else it's not good at all.

We've got to begin training ourselves to respect and honor diversity—of opinion, cultural perspective, etc. We know that the key to any system's health is its diversity, that is one of nature's fundamental principles. Our economic way of accumulation is in a sense a monoculture. How do we diversify, and find new ways to generate and distribute capital so that there is a continuous flow? How do we have the courage and compassion to live in today's painful world knowing that we very much need to create a new system? By coming face-to-face with diversity, we learn to respect what is in the present, yet imagine and create a bridge between the old and new. To create an inclusive whole, the middle path.

One of my mantras is Gandhi's dictum—to be the change that you expect in the world. The more peace I am being, the more clarity, the more awareness, health and well being there will be in my decisions about how I use each of my moments. I went into the world of nature because I knew that I could be a voice for a world that speaks a language to which few are consciously attuned. What I learned is that nature can take the best care of herself. It is we who have to learn how to take care of all the relationships within nature, including our own.

Ultimately the human species is the most endangered of all species. How do we awaken ourselves to this? We have lost connection with all the other beings on this planet, whether they appear in the forms of trees, animals, the mineral world, or the spirit realm. How do we open our psyches, cellular structure, minds, and hearts to the awesome majestic kaleidoscope of nature and be aware of it when we act, when we think, when we feel, when we make decisions? To be aware that we're not the only ones around here. The human species is the only one on this planet that accumulates more than it needs. We have not set any limits for ourselves.

At Fossil Rim, it is hoped that each event, opportunity, program, interaction with the visitor, leads to a question that one hadn't thought of before. Experiencing the impact of its awesome beauty, touching the skin of a rhino or looking at the eye of this creature that's been around for thirty million years, interacting with one of our staff, sitting in contemplation, or looking at two antelopes fight for dominance, are all experiences that lead people to connect. We hope for people to connect to what they see and experience, and therefore connect to a piece of themselves that has been denied, pushed away, erased, numbed, or forgotten. This to me is the overarching question: how do we allow our intuitions to open our hearts?

An Interview with Paul Mackay

Sometimes one gets so lost in the day-to-day details of one's financial transactions that one loses touch with some of the broader economic issues affecting daily life. Given this condition, it is refreshing to speak with an economist who can articulate with clarity some of the deep principles at play in everything from governmental monetary policy to consumer practices. As you will read in the interview, Paul Mackay has worked in international finance for many years. He has written and lectured on a wide range of economic topics, primarily in Europe. During his tenure as managing director at Triodos Bank in the Netherlands, he was involved in shaping governmental policy and legislation around finance and the environment. He brings a deep anthroposophically inspired perspective to the complicated topic of economics. I had the honor of interviewing Paul in his office in the Goetheanum, the world center for anthroposophy in Dornach, Switzerland, where he currently serves as a member of the Executive Council of the General Anthroposophical Society. He and his family live in Dornach.

This interview was conducted in June 2004.

JB: As an economist, what is your perspective on economic thinking today?

PM: Our normal way of thinking about economics should be fundamentally revised. Normally one says economics has to do with competition and having a certain market for a product. This approach is producer oriented. However, in the last decade of the last century economists began to realize that economics is really about how to manage our resources efficiently within the context of human needs wanting to be fulfilled. We are in an enormous transition in realizing that economics is not about competition but rather about fulfilling human needs in the most sensible and sustainable way. As far as I am concerned the path to sustainability is rather through cooperation than through competition. Even though this transition in thinking is underway, there's still a long way to go before the thoughts are implemented. The question is: Do we still have the time to remain in transition?

JB: Is it your sense that the economy has adjusted to limited natural resources?

PM: Due in part to the Environmental Movement in the last decades of the twentieth century, we've come to realize that resources are limited and that we have to take good care of them. For me it's an open question whether we realize this with sufficient depth and really live it, or just live with it as a question and go on with our old ways.

JB: Do you think conventional attitudes about ownership and the increasing privatization of natural resources are healthy?

PM: Such privatization is happening here in Switzerland, as well. I am quite worried about it, because certain resources are for the common good and not for private ownership. The whole ownership question should be reviewed anew because, I mean, who dares say that they own natural resources? They are God-given; they are not man-made. There's no labor activity going into the creation of these resources, and therefore they have no economic value as such. Economic value only results when labor and human activity get added to natural resources in the process of exploration. We need to discern clearly when a resource is part of the economic process and when it is not. When it is brought into the economic process, what kind of a value does it then have? What kind of price is set for it?

JB: Would drawing a distinction between what belongs in common ownership and who governs the rights of its use support the transition you mentioned?

PM: Even if one were to say that ownership is just for a specific time, then one at least moves closer to the concept of rights of use. It is important that when someone has a means of production, he or she really says, "I should use it as if it belongs to me," because then he or she will take care of it. One has to take care of one's means of production for the next generation. It doesn't really matter whether it's owned or just used; but if it's owned, the ownership should be for a limited amount of time. This approach requires a system in which the next owner is just as careful with the thing as the owner before him.

JB: Land is unique that way. With agricultural land, good farmers take care of the land because they depend upon its fertility. However, when a farmer retires, getting the capital or equity out of the farm and land is a difficult challenge. Often, farmland gets sold for development and then it leaves the agricultural realm.

PM: That happens when you have a new purpose for a piece of land, as when it goes out of farming and into project development. If I'm selling the land for project development, it commands a higher price. But why should the farmer get a huge amount of money just because he's selling the land for a different purpose? Where was the value created? By the farmer himself? Or, because the land now has a new purpose?

When value is not created out of human labor and human intelligence, then it is "virtual value," which is not real value. Virtual value is detrimental to the economy. There is quite a lot of virtual value, for instance, in the stock market. Prices go up and down, but the real value is not being expressed.

JB: Is all investment virtual value? What is the role of time in the value of money?

PM: There are two types of investment: high risk-bearing as in the stock market, and low-risk as in the bond market. If you look at the long-term development of these two markets, ultimately there's more revenue coming out of the stock market.

To invest, I have to refrain from using money for buying things. Whether I put it in the bond market, in a savings deposit, or in the stock market, the following step has been taken: I refrain from consuming now in favor of consuming at a later stage. The whole pension system is built on this concept.

Keep in mind there are two ways of financing pensions. There is the insurance way of financing pensions which is a capital-based method. This is alright to a certain extent because it makes it possible to finance the means of production. Then you have the state's way of financing pensions, which is that people now at work care for the people who are no longer able to work. As in the Social Security System, this approach is self-funding. Both ways of funding pensions are relevant. We have to take care of our fellow human beings who are living now. However, we cannot do so if we do not also work with means of production that have been financed out of a capital base.

A lot of money comes into this investment market, including all the pension money. It's enormously bloated. But the money can't go any further, so it looks primarily for more investment. This in turn generates the search for investment with the highest return. Sometimes money reaches an actual corporation or enterprise, such as when there is a new share offering, but most of the time it stays in this kind of investment market.

Since the money cannot go any further, it gets stuck there and gets older and older. Revenue is generated, but the real value is actually gone. There is no actual creation of meaningful value any more. The question is: How can we make this investment money transform itself into gift money, which is then used by people who can do research or education, who can then do all kinds of things with it, things that have an indirect but not a direct return. We still need to discover how to transform money that produces a direct return into money that has an indirect return, a gift money system.

JB: The whole pension system is based on accumulation. Are you saying that this is not value producing or healthy for the economy?

PM: It's healthy as long as what you accumulate in the capital market has real relevance to the real means of production. If there is a realistic relationship, then one doesn't get inflated price-earnings ratios. Then, I think we would have a healthy economic system. The investments that exceed the amount needed to finance the means of production could actually go into another realm. They could find their way into education and research or other such endeavors so that we have a complete cycle for human and cultural renewal.

The main instrument that we have now for this transfer is the tax system. But, nobody wants to pay taxes, so it doesn't work. I must say that in the United States there is quite a lot of money moving from the investment stage into the financing of research and education at universities. But is it enough?

JB: There is also a powerful commercial interest in and funding of university research. Is it really free or unbiased research? How might we release the energy that attaches so much power and control to money?

PM: If we create a money system that withholds money from getting stuck in the investment realm, then we would have a system in which money allows you to get a return for only a limited period of time. After that period of time, that right to the return expires. Then a lot of the power that is now in money would be removed, and much more sensible ways of using money would arise.

If every human being were conscious in buying and investing behavior, it would make an enormous difference. There are three kinds of moments when people can be conscious of their behavior about money. One is at the end of the pipeline, so to speak, where one decides whether or not to buy something that has already been produced. Investment decisions, though, are about the beginning of the pipeline, determining what kinds of things are going to be produced. In the gift money sphere one makes decisions that precede even the beginning of the pipeline, where one is influencing what capabilities are going to be developed.

JB: You are speaking of a new way of thinking about money and its uses. What drew you to economics and banking?

PM: In the late 1960s, I wanted to find out what society was all about, especially in economic life and finance. I studied economics at Rotterdam, then went to the noted business school ISEAD in France. After completing the program there, I started investment banking with ABN Amro, one of the big European banks, and was immediately promoted to the capital markets group.

That was in the early 1970s. Quite a lot was happening in those years—we got off the gold standard, off fixed parities with exchange rates, and, in 1973, we also had the Yom Kippur War in Israel. This shifted the whole world economy because, as a result of that war, oil prices went up. I saw what a powerful effect it had on the capital markets, particularly as the global and developing countries' markets were emerging.

JB: Eventually you started an anthroposophical bank.

PM: Yes, but there was an intermission before that. After having been in investment banking for a number of years, I came to the inner question of whether I should take a break. I remembered that at university I had a professor, Bernard Lievegoed, who had made quite an impression on me. I renewed my contact with him, and then discovered he was an anthroposophist. Through him I found out about an upcoming workshop on social development, which I took a leave to attend.

That workshop was at Emerson College in England. The idea to set up the Center for Social Development arose during that workshop. I got quite excited about anthroposophy, and spent most of my time in the library speed-reading Rudolf Steiner's works. I left my banking work to study anthroposophy for more than two years, mostly in Stuttgart, Germany, at the seminary of the Christian Community.

During the time I was at the seminary, someone told me about an anthroposophical bank in Bochum, Germany, the Gemeinschaftsbank, and suggested it might be something for me because of my banking background. I was not interested then.

Two years later, through a friend, I was introduced to the Gemeinschaftsbank. They invited me to join, and eventually I accepted. At the same time, I started working with a group that wanted to found a bank in the Netherlands. I was working on two things at the same time. That was in 1977. We spent three years preparing the foundation of the Triodos Bank in the Netherlands. In 1983, a year after Triodos was set up, I was invited to join as managing director. Off I went to Holland.

JB: So what were some of the challenges there? Was there a tension between the mission of the bank and creating a broad market for it?

PM: I personally had a major responsibility for getting the business going. From the start, Triodos Bank was very much in the public eye. When the Triodos Bank started, there was a press conference, people were excited. There was much more public interest than there had been in Germany. The Gemeinschaftsbank primarily served the anthroposophical movement, whereas with Triodos Bank there was public interest from the start. It is also more commercially oriented.

JB: We have been addressing broad economic issues, but how can I as an individual influence the economy through how I use my money? What can I do on a daily basis as a consumer, for example?

PM: If each person would be conscious in his or her buying and investing behavior, it would make an enormous difference. For example, if no one buys an item that is stocked on the shelves of a store, the storekeeper will decide not to order or carry that item any more. That affects what will be produced, and at the same time also conditions where investment is made. The collective action of many individuals can have great impact on production and the marketplace.

JB: From your perspective what do you think are the financial challenges for America?

PM: For decades there's been a balance of payments deficit in the U.S. It is huge and growing. And, what is a balance of payments deficit? It results from spending more than your income. Right after World War II, this was no problem because the dollar was the world currency. The dollar is still the currency that drives world trade. But the question is whether that will go on or change.

There is a challenge for the U.S. to be more responsible for the value of the dollar. Based on how that is managed, the world economy could develop in different ways. First, each national "household" has to come into order and balance. What I'm saying applies not just to the U.S., but also to every other country. Is there a balance between what one gets out of the economy and what one puts into it? Am I living off the economy, or am I contributing enough to the economy?

For instance, if I look at China now, they are growing now as Japan was in the 1960s and 1970s. I have a feeling there is a quality of "young productivity" surfacing in China. There are other developed countries that are also striving for this quality. But, at least for Europe, I believe it is not our task to have a young productivity, but rather to have an old productivity. In an old productivity, one has to create value that is different in quality than the value being created in "tiger" countries like China or Taiwan.

I know if we in Europe go on producing things that could be better produced in developing countries, then we will not have a healthy economy. We have to look for things that are uniquely produced here in Europe, that add value for the world at large.

We have to distinguish which countries are making what contributions. I wonder what the unique contribution of the U.S. is for the world at large. The U.S. has a unique contribution to make, and shouldn't fall back into making the same contributions it did decades ago, to the detriment of developing new things. For one example of where there is innovation, look at the wonderful universities in the U.S. There is an intellectual capacity there that is not available in other countries. Recognizing and supporting the gifts that each culture brings to the world economy is the greatest international challenge. I have a strong sense that people are waking up to those challenges and trying to find new ways of working together that also respect our limited natural resources. However, there is always great resistance to change.

JB: Does it seem likely that there will be a single world currency?

PM: I cannot imagine a singular world currency at this moment. We are not ready for it. One could say a world currency is theoretically of interest because it makes a level playing field on which it is no longer possible to gain advantage over another country's economy just by changing the exchange rate. This is what we are now learning in Europe. We have the Euro as the single currency in Europe. Consequently, no one European country can create a competitive export advantage over another within the European community by lowering the value of its currency.

At this moment in time, the Euro has the potential to become a world currency alongside the U.S. dollar. This would be a step forward, because the economic responsibility that the U.S. took up after World War II should be shared now. This is one more aspect of the fundamental economic restructuring that is unfolding in the world economy.

An Interview with Michael Spence

Economics is one of three sectors of social life as articulated by Rudolf Steiner in his writings and lectures on the threefold commonwealth. This social theory is an extraordinary tool for transforming how we view and conduct life in a civil society. But it is also challenging to understand. Michael Spence is one of the first people I met who could convey a coherent sense of the theory, and demonstrate how it could be applied practically in an organization such as an independent school.

Prior to joining Emerson College in England, where he served as bursar for twenty-seven years, he worked in the finance industry, encouraging the auto and farm machinery businesses to finance their customers. Emerson College, an adult education center devoted to furthering Rudolf Steiner's work in education, agriculture and other fields, was Michael's demonstration laboratory. His experience there, in addition to his work preparing lectures and workshops on aspects of money, formed the basis for his book, *Freeing the Human Spirit*, which focused on the financial life of Waldorf schools based on threefold social concepts. He has since completed a manuscript for his next book, *After Capitalism*, which more broadly applies these concepts to our current economic climate.

This interview was conducted in January 2000.

JB: What have you been working on since completing your book, *Freeing the Human Spirit*?

MS: Writing that book challenged me to refine and organize ideas that I had written or lectured about in many different places. Coming here to America, I met a lot of people who had deep questions about the practicality of the threefold social ideas, questions that I didn't find back in Europe. I've returned to my original intention of writing for a wider public now, and in that I go much more deeply into many aspects of money, economic outcome, and investments, such as what is land ownership, what is share ownership. I only just touch on these in *Freeing the Human Spirit*.

JB: These are very complicated topics because there are so many factors involved. Perhaps you could address the investment question first.

MS: First of all, how has ownership arisen? How is it that one can own land, or can own a share in a company? Why is it that ownership of that share takes precedent over the person who works in the factory? And, precedent over the person who needs and buys the products of the factory? The profit goes to the owner, not the maker. How has this situation arisen? It really has arisen out of the type of law that goes back to a different time when there was a paternalistic society with its aristocracy, landowners, and the people who were virtually slaves. The primary difference now is that you buy the labor.

JB: Sounds like a picture of feudal life.

MS: A lot of our law comes out of feudal times. If we had to create law today with our modern democratic way of thinking, would we arrive at the same law? After all, law is something that is created by human beings, not gods. What we have created, we can change. We can ask, is this the kind of law we want? If it is changed, the whole structure of economic life will change with it.

JB: You seem to be addressing the essential social question of the relationship between money and power.

MS: That arises out of it. I see two sources of money. One source of money is when someone produces something that's needed and sells it. In that production, money is absolutely essential because it needs to be saved and used as capital to stock new things. The second source of money, which has nothing to do with the first, treats ownership or rights as an economic product. Consequently, you've got two economies—the economy of products and the economy of rights and ownership. Copyrights or permission to extract metals or minerals are examples of this latter form of economy. This is the linkage between the economy and rights, between money and power. But, is that how rights should be allocated—to those who can afford to buy them?

JB: It really raises the question of intellectual property. How, for example, can one own an idea?

MS: It raises many questions. Although I can see rights working in a different way, the question is how could it come about differently? There are already many people and organizations that realize things could be better. First, land should not be subject purely to buying and selling. One has to consider the people who need access to the land. The land of a people should be allocated on a different basis than just being able to buy it. Rather, it should be on a basis of who can use it best, or whose use of the land would best benefit the community.

There's an element here of the old common law in England. Up until very recently we had no such law as trespass. Anyone could walk over the land. Disruption or damages were offenses, but walking over the land was considered normal and natural use. The land belonged to the Crown in common.

If a person planted or in any way cared for something, then that was his. However, blossoms or fruit that originated naturally, that were nurtured by nature rather than by the hand of the farmer, anyone could pick. As soon as the farmer cares for it, it's his.

JB: There's a quality of human attention and intention in this system of rights.

MS: Human action, too. The focus is on the value and consequence of work. You've pruned and watered the tree. You own the consequence of your action, since the tree is improved by it—you have a right to the crop. Ownership of the tree is another question. As far as I know, if you have planted it then it's yours. A barrister who studied these things once told me that in the working of the law, one can really say that your ownership of land actually hovers over the land. It doesn't include the substance of the land. In English law, you have the right to use the land, but you don't own the land.

JB: In that view, it is almost as if ownership is metaphysical.

MS: Yes, and it's something created purely by law. There are many cultures that do not recognize ownership as a concept, except in a collective sense. A tribe or people might control and use the land, but ownership was often vested in a king or other symbolic leader. For instance, in England, mineral rights are referred to as Crown Property, owned by the government on behalf of the people.

JB: How would you characterize investment in land, property, and the products made from them?

MS: There are many different types of investments. One investment is when you lend your hard-earned or saved money to someone who's got a good idea. This loan makes it possible for that person to establish a workshop and bring those ideas into production. This might be a better way of making shoes, or a new technology. Unless the person gets the tools and the money, the idea remains in his or her head and is no good to anyone. Investment in this sense can be a real service in releasing human capacity.

A second kind of investment is one that merely plays, for instance, on the increase in value of shares or land. You may have bought some shares on the belief that they're going to rise in value. You later sell those shares at that higher value. In this case the money doesn't actually go into the business. Those shares go up in value, the dividend goes up, and you live on the proceeds, while other people have been laboring in production toward which you've contributed nothing. The original share might have cost a dollar and is now worth thirty dollars. Twenty-nine dollars have gone to other people who have owned shares at different times. Only the first dollar went to the company. You may also get a dividend on thirty dollars because the value of the company has gone up. Your money hasn't gone into the company, and has no effect on their production.

You get more than you originally paid, so you benefit from the capital increase. Then I benefit from the capital increase. But one day, somehow or other, this has got to be paid for. You spend that capital, pay for something, buy the products of someone's work with money that has no objective value behind it. There are three possible ways that will be paid for. One is in the future when there's a financial crash or these stock prices actually come down again. Then it's paid for by the people who lose money, or by inflation, or it's paid for by a distortion in the prices of goods and what people are paid for the products of their work. In that case, people are actually being paid less than the true value of the products of their work and the work they produce. This is very complex from the perspective of the division of labor. Very often the people at lower levels are actually producing the things that everybody needs, including for the people at a higher level. The people at a higher level are not actually producing anything at all. That difference is paid for by an overvaluation of investments. Speculation creates fluctuations in the value, but overall there is an increase over time. Indices such as Dow-Jones reflect this pattern of increase. I want to look at this phenomenon from a purely objective point of view, so that I can separate the two kinds of economies I've described.

JB: If money and its value generate themselves separately from a direct connection to productivity, is labor then devalued or degraded as a capacity?

MS: To me it doesn't degrade labor as such. Labor should be deeply respected. The people who do the physical work are often subservient to the people who are able to increase the amount of money. They are servants in the sense that they manufacture what these people want. Power and wealth are being held in fewer and fewer hands. Historically, in the old theocracies, the monarchies, the aristocracies, or even the religions, these were times when a few had power over many. We're coming back to this condition in an even greater degree. Only when you've got money are you in a position to get more money.

JB: That sheds an interesting light on the concept of the minimum wage.

MS: I want to address the concept of wage and salary from a new perspective. What is the basis of wage out of which the concept of minimum wage comes? What is a wage? What will wages look like in the future? I am sure the whole concept of wages will change, just as slavery as an economic basis had to change. A time will come when people will say you can't buy labor. In the year 4,000, they will ask how, two thousand years ago, you could have had an economy based on buying labor. They will realize the meaning of the concept that the human is free, that money will serve to free human capacity rather than govern it. You don't buy labor, just as you don't buy slaves. I'm convinced that you will see signs of this in many different ways—an impulse to move away from the purchase of labor into other forms of economic support. That's got to come.

I haven't spent much time researching credit as such. Economic life, particularly its financial aspect, is immensely complex, so one can only follow certain strands through it. What interests me enormously is the whole intricacy and mystery of the division of labor. It is the basis of all economic production. What does the division of labor mean?

We each look after ourselves. I want to make myself a pair of sandals, which requires an enormous amount of work—especially if I've got to make the tools and produce the leather and everything else. I also want to make a shirt, which is also going to be an enormous amount of work. I discover that you also want to make yourself a pair of sandals and a shirt. Then out of our discussion we determine that I will make myself a pair of sandals, but instead of making a shirt, I'll make a second pair of sandals for you. And while you're making your shirt, you make a second shirt for me. And as soon as we do that, your second shirt and my second pair of sandals are enormously simpler to make than the first pair, because I've already got the tools and the know-how. I make the second pair of sandals and I exchange them for the shirt. I give something that I made fairly simply, and I get something back that would have been more complex for me to make. We each profit, we gain. What is really at the core of this exchange is that as soon as I make sandals for you, the whole thing improves. It's more productive, more effective, saves time, and saves work. I still get my shirt but I get it by making a pair of sandals for you. That is the basis of the division of labor. As soon as you cease to make it for yourself, but rather make it for the other people, you create an enormously productive economy.

JB: The traditional view of the division of labor is a much more mechanistic one, in that each person has his or her place in the economy, like a part in a machine. There is a hierarchy there, in that manual labor is not as valued as management. This is a different kind of division of labor than you are talking about.

MS: It comes out of the same reality, but it's been embraced in a different way. The division of labor is more than just a separation of functions; it also represents the transformation of thought. Let me give you an example of a mechanical crane. When you come onto a building site, you can watch the crane at work, lifting its huge weight to the top of the building. Imagine if that had to be lifted up purely by human hands. You can talk about the cable lifting it or the engine pulling the cable or the fuel burning in the engine or the fire—but you come eventually to human thought. You could say it's human thought that makes the lifting possible. Human thought is making work more effective.

Here is another thought. As you're washing up the dishes, you might ask who is actually washing up. Imagine if I had to go down to the river to collect the water, and wood to light a fire to heat it with, and then wash my dishes—but I don't. There are other people collecting the water, others heating it by generating electricity. A million other people and I are doing the washing up. That is division of labor or the consequences of it.

Look at a crane again, at the individual parts, the nuts, the bolts. From this you can come to the thought that every bit of it is substance-filled human thought. It's all been thought through and planned. That's what lifts the weight, it's the thought, ultimately.

JB: It is ironic that we now argue that some aspects of technology, the electronic media for instance, are damaging our thinking capacity.

MS: It is the story of the sorcerer's apprentice—that age-old story where the apprentice tries to take on the work of the master. But, he's not learned to handle the tools properly, and the tools take over. We haven't developed the inner discipline, the inner strength, to know when to use these possibilities and when they've become destructive. Although we're creating many things now that are not really needed, computers are powerful and useful. It's not that the technology is wrong, but rather our capacity to control it, or letting it take over our will.

JB: Is there a moral issue there?

MS: If one means the morals of good and bad, then I would hesitate to use the word "moral." If one is using moral in the sense of what is true to my own deeper nature, or the deeper spiritual nature of the individual, of what will enable human beings to become what they must become, then, yes, it's a highly moral question.

JB: What is the relationship between the cultural life and the economic life?

MS: I see the cultural life as leading to the point and economic life leading to the periphery. Individuals have to find the truth for themselves. I can lead you to ideas, tell you what I've found as true, but only you can confirm or accept for yourself whether they are true or not. There's no division of labor in cultural life because we are actually independent in our thinking.

Economic life contains cultural life—the workings of creativity and imagination are really cultural life working into economic life. In one sense, that is one-half the division of labor. Human thoughts arise out of cultural life and flow into the economic. Rudolf Steiner refers to this as the half-free cultural life. Because you're caught up in the laws of production, you're not entirely free and yet you're creative. The creativity that produced the crane is the other extreme from actual physical labor within economic life. It's the part that comes from cultural life—creativity, engineering, design—into economic life that gives rise to specialization.

I would say the engineer is working out of cultural life into the economic life, because he's creating the crane that is going to lift the loads to help build the building. His creativity has to die into substance, so to speak. The artists on the other hand, are awakening a capacity within themselves and other human beings. This is a living and renewing process rather than a dying one and is purely cultural.

It is a dynamic balance between cultural life and economic life. Ideas and imaginations move from cultural life into economic life. The products of economic life flow into cultural life to make it possible, for example, for education to happen, for the teacher to work with the child. For this they need a building, chalk, and paper. Economic life provides this. Thus, there is an extraordinary balance and movement between these two extremes—at the center point the individual, and at the other extreme, the periphery, world humanity. It is a beautiful interweaving between these polarities.

An Interview with an Lynne Twist

Lynne Twist published her award-winning book *The Soul of Money: Transforming Your Relationship with Money and Life* in 2003. The paperback came out in 2006. The book itself is full of engaging stories drawn from her extensive and profound life experience around money and changing the world. The stories range from her work as founding staff member of The Hunger Project in 1977 to her recent work in preserving the rain forest of southern Ecuador through the Pachamama Alliance, which she co-founded with her husband in 1995. Most recently she started The Soul of Money Institute to further the dialogue on money and to help build a community of interest in this topic so central to our time.

Her accomplishments are many, far too numerous to list in a short introduction. And, one can explore www.soulofmoney.org to find out more about her life. What is not listed there though is what is immediately evident when one meets her in person—her extraordinary passion and energy, clarity of purpose, and ability to be fully present despite the many demands on her life and time. When quite the opposite would be possible, she is full of humility and she stands totally in a position of service to the world, much as an instrument is to music. She has brought her life experience and capacity for insight to this interview.

This interview was conducted in November 2003.

JB: Did you ever imagine that you would be so involved with money when you were growing up?

LT: I had several flashes in my life that I know started to steer me in this direction. Once when I was a little girl, I suddenly realized that everybody wasn't happy, and that there were some children who were starving. I was totally shocked, and I wanted to know why adults would let that happen. I remember thinking: "this isn't right and some day, when I grow up, I'll do something about it."

Then, the day before my thirteenth birthday, my father died. He was an orchestra leader, a vivacious man. Music filled our house all the time. He and I played two pianos together. We were very close. He had a heart attack in the middle of the night. It was so shocking, with no warning. It was just so illogical that my dad would be taken away, that at some level of my being, I thought I'd done something wrong, and that God had taken my dad away.

In response, I became very, very religious. I started going to mass every single day and I thought about becoming a nun. I became deeply devoted to Christ and to the Virgin Mary. All of that became my private world. At the same time, I was really popular. I was the cheerleader, head of the pom-pom section, president of my high school. I was homecoming queen. I was dating the football star. I was one of those kids that did everything.

I had a very public life, but I didn't want anybody to know that I was going to mass every day, so I also had a double life. I went to mass early in the morning, before my friends came and picked me up. I had a private relationship with God that was profound. A lot of it was driven by this underlying guilt about my dad's death. I wanted to do something to make up for it. I also realized that I wanted to make my father proud.

College was another turning point. I had this longing to get married and have children, but I also had the notion that I could really make a difference with my life. When I got to Stanford, where my father had gone, my religious life started to fade a little, and I got involved in poetry. My spiritual relationship was expressed through the world of poetry, which I found so profound. That was another turning point in my spiritual development. Then, I did get married. My husband and I have one of those relationships that you think is only possible in the movies. Now, 37 years later, my relationship with my husband is part of my spiritual path.

Everybody has milestones and epiphanies. Mine came in the EST training, which I took in 1974 with Werner Erhard. It just revolutionized my life. I really came to understand that I could turn my life over to making a difference. That experience led me to be in the right place at the right time when The Hunger Project was born. I heard Werner Erhard say for the first time at a big meeting that he was taking a stand to end world hunger. My whole body started to shake, and I knew that that was why I was born, that that was what I came here to do. It was impractical because I was a very busy young mother, but it was a calling so remarkable that I could not deny it, and so I went with it.

JB: Would you say that was the time in which your inner and outer lives were reconciled or integrated?

LT: That's what the EST training did for me. What you've just articulated is exactly right. What was almost a split personality, between my spiritual path and my more public path, became one. I became fearless about living authentically after the EST training. Then The Hunger Project gave me the platform to express it.

JB: You mean in terms of visible, results-oriented work?

LT: Yes. The Hunger Project catapulted me into a global commitment with significant ramifications and broad dimensions. I took a stand with my life. You know Archimedes said "give me a place to stand and I'll move the world." That's what happened to me; I found a place to stand where I could actually make a contribution that would move the world. That was the great blessing of The Hunger Project for me.

JB: That project served as a home base, but it also sounds like it was a spiritual home.

LT: Absolutely. However, we didn't use spiritual language in The Hunger Project. The Hunger Project is now and always has been about the physical hunger and death of children and women and old men, as well as about the inner hunger that exists as a spiritual crisis in the affluent nations and the human heart. The Hunger Project was and continues to be a very spiritual path for me.

JB: In your book, *Soul of Money*, you made a number of references to the laws of the natural world which you link to *sufficiency*, an important theme in your work. How do you link the laws of the natural world with money?

LT: Well, my awakening about the natural world really came through the encounter with the Achuar people in the south Ecuadorean region of the Amazon. That is another place in my life where I've had what I would call an epiphany. When I worked on hunger and poverty, I was focused on human life in a way that was almost separate from the natural environment. It was through the good fortune of being invited to meet with the Achuar people, and my partnership with John Perkins, the great shamanic teacher and a colleague of mine, that I realized that I had a blind spot in my relationship with the natural world.

I saw in the rain forest the absolute perfection and prosperity of the natural system—the beauty of the decay and the death of this tree or this animal. This is not waste, but the beginning of the next creature or next form of life. It's so obvious and palpable, that there's no waste in the rain forest, that competition is appropriate. Those plants and animals that survive are the ones that actually collaborate. This lawfulness became so clear to me walking through the forest with the indigenous people. I also started to understand why, in their world, the indigenous people didn't have any money. It wasn't a part of their world, they just shared everything. There was no ownership. The commons and communal values were much higher than individual values. Everybody made everything work for everybody else. That is the security of the way of life there.

Seeing everything working so beautifully in the forest, and, seeing the people mirroring that, validated all my earlier notions about this idea of *sufficiency*— that there is enough. It also prepared me to understand why introducing money into that society, which has now happened, is very confusing because the money system is based on scarcity. To have the indigenous people have a successful encounter with money continues to be one of the great challenges of our work in the rain forest through The Pachamama Alliance, which my husband and I founded. I began to see how important it is to relate to money differently, not to get caught in the scarcity model.

I can see how important it is to make our financial structures like the rain forest, where there's competition as appropriate to forward the evolution of life.

Alongside competition are the power, beauty and excellence that come from collaboration and surrender. Money is just the instrument that we've invented to allow us to share with one another. We need to have both competition and collaboration; we need to temper scarcity with the experience of sufficiency.

JB: Could you define *sufficiency* as you see it? There is a history and philosophical lineage behind the concepts of sufficiency, abundance and scarcity.

LT: I talk about sufficiency as almost a declaration of being. Sufficiency is a grounded being, a way of seeing the world where we see that resources are finite, but they are *enough*. That makes resources precious rather than scarce. That puts us in a relationship of reverence with the resources we have, rather than a relationship of fear because they are being depleted. The principle of sufficiency is that you let go of trying to get more of what you don't really need, which in turn frees up oceans of energy to focus our attention to making a difference with what we do have. When you make a difference with what you have, it naturally expands. I think that's a law of sufficiency, that when you turn your attention and your presence to the exquisite experience of *enough*, which I think is an experience of perfection, of being totally in the now, of gratitude and blessing, then everything that you give that attention to begins to expand. As I say in my book, "what you appreciate appreciates."

Sufficiency is the doorway to prosperity and fulfillment. I don't think you can get to the same place through the doorway of *more*. Sufficiency is also the portal to abundance. In order to release the scarcity mindset, one needs to experience that magnificent perfection of *enough*, and from there abundance flows.

JB: One of the great American ideals articulated by Ralph Waldo Emerson is self-reliance. This concept is tied to sufficiency and even to self-sufficiency. But as you outline it, any kind of money assures that one can't be self-sufficient, or, more positively, that one lives in a system of interdependence. One doesn't usually think of sufficiency as a condition of the soul, and yet your whole book is about the soul of money and achieving sufficiency. How is it that such a wide range of people are interested in and included under the *Soul of Money* umbrella?

LT: If you ask me what my soul is, I have no idea what it is or where it is, but it's different from spirit. It is in the center of the center of the center of the experience of life. It's at the deepest place in my being and it encompasses everything.

JB: Where does money link to that experience?

LT: I've had such an unexpected, amazing path with money, which has taken me deep into the soul of humanity. It is an unexpected route, but interacting with people about their money with heart and authenticity, has led me into the heart of people's soul. This is what people really end up talking to me about when I'm fundraising. I've been so blessed in some of these encounters and interactions in which people have felt safe enough with me and I've felt safe enough with them for us to go kind of beyond where most relationships go. I have been extremely fortunate that money and development work have been instruments, vehicles or the pathways that have made possible such a remarkable set of experiences interacting with people in the most soulful way.

JB: As you describe it, money is almost a form of expressive speech or poetry across the relationship.

LT: Money is a carrier, a conduit, a current or a currency that carries the soul, or can. It's not always that. It can bear revenge, retribution, domination and hatred. When it carries those it can be just absolutely brutal and lethal. When it carries the soul it really is food for the world of the best kind.

The most recent chapter of my life, working with indigenous people in the Amazon, has been completely miraculous. I knew nothing about environmental issues and ecology. Even though my experiences had not prepared me for it, they completely prepared me for it, because everything that I learned in other settings has been affirmed by the exquisite wisdom of indigenous people. They have been such an important gift and are my newest and most profound teachers.

They tell a prophecy of the Eagle and the Condor. It says that the Eagle people, who are the people of the mind at this point in evolution, like you and me, will have developed their mind to such a zenith that they will have attained material wealth beyond their wildest dreams. But they will be spiritually impoverished to their peril, and their very survival will be at risk. The Condor people, who are the indigenous people, will be highly evolved in the ways of the spirit, the body, the heart and the senses, and they will know the natural world intimately and in a very sophisticated way. But, they will be materially impoverished to their peril, especially in any encounter with the Eagle, and their very survival will be at risk. The prophecy tells that now is the time when the Eagle and the Condor will remember that they are one, and will fly together in the same sky wing to wing, and the world will come back into balance.

And the indigenous people that we worked with, the Achuar people in particular, have told us that our work in the rain forest with The Pachamama Alliance is the world coming back into balance. In their prophecies and dreams they've seen that they will prevail, that they will turn the tide—and I feel very encouraged by that.

JB: I wonder if the *Soul of Money* is the beginning of another turning point in your life because of the focus on the money question.

LT: Because of the book, I'm out in the general public. And, the general public, by the way, is just wonderful. In Cincinnati, Chicago, and Minneapolis, in all of all these places, people are completely awake, and they're unsettled, they're at work and they're questioning. I'm so inspired by my fellow Americans! I don't have the feeling any more that people are asleep and we all need to wake them up. Rather that there is enormous opportunity for a dialogue.

JB: Because you write and speak about money, you create permission and a language for others to speak about money and their experiences with it. The native wisdom, interest, and need for this dialogue are there. It just somehow or other hasn't had a place to surface. If you're discovering that your book has tapped into that, and your presence has allowed that to come forth, then it is a real and transformative gift to the world.

LT: Because of the EST training and The Hunger Project, I got clear on the distinction early enough in my life between *taking a stand* and *taking a position*. That has been critical in my journey, because I've chosen to take a stand, and a stand includes all positions. It makes none of them wrong, whereas a position calls up its *opposition*. People like Martin Luther King and Gandhi were stand-takers. That's why their wisdom is still palpable today. When you take a stand, you are given the real privilege of living a committed life, in which the word that you've given is what directs you. Your wants and your desires pale. A stand is always *for* life, it's never *against* anything, yet it guides you toward the truth. I'm so fortunate that I learned that in my early thirties so I could live my life with that knowledge. I don't always live up to it, of course, but it's something I know to be true.

An Interview with Betsy Taylor

Change is challenging for anyone, and even greater for organizations and systems. Yet changing our lives for a better future is essentially what Betsy Taylor and the Center for the New American Dream are about. What is asked for is that we be awake to our highest values and start living accordingly. Betsy Taylor and her founding colleagues, including the inspiring environmentalist Donella Meadows and economist and author Juliet Schor, recognized that we are at a cultural and environmental turning point that calls for positive transformation. Their primary field of activity is our lives as consumers, believing that conscious consuming will leverage the whole economic system toward social and environmental justice. Ms. Taylor is president of 1Sky, and past president of the Center for the New American Dream, founded in 1998. She was formerly executive director of Merck Family Fund and vice-chair of the Environmental Grant-makers Association. She is author of *What Kids Really Want that Money Can't Buy* and co-editor of *Sustainable Planet: Solutions for the 21st Century*. She has written op-ed articles, spoken before the United Nations, served as a member of the Population and Consumption Taskforce for the President's Council on Sustainable Development, managed many campaigns and policy initiatives, and most recently has been a commentator on National Public Radio.

I came to know the Center for the New American Dream as part of RSF Social Finance's Transforming Money Network. We deeply appreciate the extraordinary impact the organization has already had on patterns of consumptions and for their ability to form an inviting community in common cause for humanity and the environment. Ms. Taylor is an enthusiastic proponent for our ability to bring about change in a healthy way by simply trusting in the guidance of our inner voice. One cannot help but be engaged in a thorough re-evaluation of one's life after meeting with her.

This interview was conducted in October 2004.

JB: Why did you and your co-founders decide to name the new organization The Center for the New American Dream?

BT: We were aspiring to a new vision, a new way to frame our collective imagination of how the world could be. We were all reacting to the definition of the American Dream that emerged in the 1980s and 90s. Then it was more like a luxury fever. By calling it the New American Dream, we wanted to put the mission of our new Center in the tradition of the original American Dream, to reclaim some of the early values associated with the Dream, and then redefine it as something other than one focused on the self and individualism above all else.

This New American Dream allowed us to embrace the multiple dimensions and consequences of excessive consumption in an integrated way. The more one goes into these dimensions, the more one can see the significance of the Center's many themes: the environment, economic justice, quality of life, and the fundamental existential and spiritual questions of why we are here.

JB: Can you say more about the traditional view of the American Dream? Are there particular aspects you are trying to bring to light?

BT: Most Americans assume that, given a supportive environment with adequate opportunities, with hard work, with the freedom to live their hopes, they could have a reasonably good life. That was part of the original concept. From the early days of American history, it was also coupled with a ferocious commitment to the separation of church and state.

The formative American Dream was also a reaction to excess. Some of the early settlers were reacting against the excess that was dominating both the church and, in some cases, the state in several European countries. There was also a commitment to a can-do spirit—the sense that people are meant for, in part, adventure and for some bold purpose in life. As we were imagining the Center, we wanted to hold on to a lot of that.

No question, there were also material aspirations from the start. In recent years, Madison Avenue and the advertising industry have completely commercialized the American dream. It is now overwhelmingly about acquisition and getting ahead. We have also taken individualism to a radical extreme, leaving people feeling very alone in a highly turbulent economy and world. This is wearing a lot of people out, and not leading to the quality of life or genuine security that people really hope for.

JB: The *Art Director's Annual* for 1955 stated: "It is now the business of advertising to manufacture customers in the comfort of their own homes." Is this the intentional commercialization you are referring to?

BT: As soon as television landed in the living room, we began having manufactured desires. Now this happens not only in the living room, but also the internet, on our clothing. The messages are everywhere. We are being programmed for discontent.

JB: If commercial messages are so pervasive why are we not numb or immune to them by now?

BT: Most Americans say that advertising doesn't affect them. But if you actually look at empirical studies, it profoundly affects them. It is the background noise of our daily lives. In some ways we do get numb. I think many people don't even see them anymore, but the messages are there all the time—in schools, fashion, magazines, billboards, radio, TV. Together, these messages add up to convince us that security, fulfillment and happiness are found through consuming and that more is just never enough.

JB: How does the Center counter or challenge that influence?

BT: We're building a movement of people who live consciously, buy wisely, and work to change the system. The agenda that we're challenging is the culture that celebrates excessive materialism, and economic processes that institutionalize greed. Many, many Americans are troubled by this. The Center just conducted a poll: 93 percent of Americans say that we're too focused on working and spending and not enough on family life and community—nine out of ten Americans think our priorities are out of whack—that's, almost everybody!

Several historical and cultural threads have come together at the same time to propel us to work and spend more. We've been through several revolutionary changes within a period of a few decades. One is the change in the global commerce. The rules of business have changed in a dramatic fashion to reward companies that go global. This has had profound effects on us. Those companies operate with intensive branding and marketing at a global scale so that children in Bangkok and Los Angeles become tied together through a "swoosh." Youth and adults are besieged with ads from these companies, from McDonalds to Sony, urging them to buy more. We have also had a technological revolution. Suddenly, everybody's hooked up. With that technology and information has come great wealth—the largest acquisition of wealth since the beginning of the twentieth century.

A centerpiece of this period has been a celebration of wealth, and a glorification of consumption. You see it everywhere in the media, the theme of get-rich-quick. Wealth in itself is not bad. But we are glorifying millionaires (and hoping to marry them). We are celebrating the lifestyles of the rich and famous and in this cultural context of luxury fever, many people feel great pressure to buy and do more, just to feel "okay." Furthermore, when the pursuit or acquisition of wealth comes in ways that are demeaning, or generates greater injustice, everyone is hurt. On some deep value level, people know this and know that it does not feel right.

JB: How do you acknowledge that sense of rightness and support the ability to change circumstances?

BT: The vast majority of Americans feel that our country is going in the wrong direction, but they don't have a place to talk about it or a way to find other like-minded people. People want to live according to their deepest values and yet they find it really difficult. The culture is hostile to it—especially for parents trying to raise conscious, healthy children.

JB: Are there growing communities that share these kinds of values?

BT: Ten years ago, people felt alone and isolated. There are now a lot of people who share these values. The Center will have close to two million distinct visitors on our website this year, people searching for ways to have more fun with less stuff, to consume wisely, and to be part of challenging the "more is better definition" of happiness. We are creating a place where people have some support and tools to come together. It's hard to live consciously if you are entirely isolated from others.

JB: Money can be an isolating force. Is this part of the challenge you are meeting?

BT: The extraordinary pressure to get more, to accumulate it—people's status and identity have become increasingly bound to it. We've always had identity coming from objects and wealth to some extent, but it's just gotten completely out of balance in recent years.

JB: The pressure for that kind of identity has been encouraged and fed with increasing sophistication through the creation of the marketplace.

BT: It's constantly fed. *Business Week* said we get about 3000 commercial messages a day coming at us; it's just there all the time, pulsing. Even if you don't watch commercial television, it's still coming at you in a variety of ways. To counter the pressure, the first step is to simply unplug from the dominant media-driven culture. Turn off the commercial television. Ignore the Internet for long periods of time. Be in nature. Be quiet. That's a prerequisite for listening to your inner voice and for developing clarity about the kind of life you really want to live. As people work to unplug and live consciously, most find they are drawn to the larger questions about the system. This work is both about helping people secure greater personal fulfillment but also about meeting one of the greatest moral challenges of our times.

JB: In what sense do you mean a moral challenge?

BT: Many people approach us because their lives don't feel right and we support them in making choices to live differently—to consume less, work less, and seek more joy from non-material sources. As they get into the conversation, they see that there are implications of consumption far greater than themselves—implications that extend to everything from national security to environmental survival. A big part of our work is to help folks to realize that the pursuit of the good life is also deeply connected to the pursuit of social justice, environmental safety, and security.

Americans consume 30% of the world's material resources and 40% of the world's gasoline. If we can reduce consumption, we can help the environment, reduce our dependence on Middle East oil, improve relations with other nations, and address the extraordinary inequity between the northern and southern hemispheres. Increasingly we are finding people are connecting these dots—seeking balance for themselves but also balance for the earth and its peoples.

When we go into this question of consumption, it touches on all of these issues. With the New American Dream, part of what we are trying to contribute, not exclusively or wholly, is to say: we can have a different structure for work; we can have a different kind of safety net; we can consume less; have more time; have more material security. Look, it doesn't have to be structured this way. Right now we have the highest level ever of global unemployment. We need to reduce the work week and share the work. We have the highest level ever of inequity, with 20% of the world consuming 80% of the resources. We need to share. We live in a fearful world—the number one emotional feeling worldwide right now is anxiety. Why not take some of our money, our collective resources, to provide the safety net that would make everyone slow down, feel safer, work less, enjoy life more, feel secure, avoid war, and so forth.

I don't want to overstate our contribution to the new progressive vision. However, people are hungry for solutions—not just for rightness, but for solutions. They are hungry for hope. They are hungry for the belief that their kids are actually going to be okay. There is not a lot of that being offered up right now.

To find those solutions, we actually have to face some of the paradoxes in our current situation. Politicians and economists especially seem ill-equipped to face this. Consumption is right at the heart of it. In the final presidential debate, both John Kerry and George Bush specifically named consumption as the key to our future prosperity. At the same time, you have scientists screaming for reduction of consumption because the glaciers are melting, half the amphibians are expected to be gone in 20 years, along with 30 percent of the birds in 15 years. Global unemployment is rising, so it is increasingly taboo to talk about anything being wrong with consumption because that is what they say will keep the wealth and job generation going. There are some really fundamental economic principles and practices that need to change. We really need a different economic paradigm.

JB: What do you think has driven people to spend so much and to carry so much debt?

BT: They have been encouraged to. Right after 9/11, the first thing we were told to do was to go shop. President Bush specifically spoke to that. It was a very strange moment. When people were reaching out and wanting to help—wanting to come together, to transcend the mundane, they were told to go to the mall to make sure that nothing fell apart in the market.

   Why so much debt? Our approach to credit in this country is different than in Europe, for example. There is far more predatory lending here. Many of the people who are in debt are immigrants or young people. One-fourth of college students are in trouble with credit card debt. It is staggering the number of people who are just a couple of months away from bankruptcy. The way credit is offered to consumers is very much "buy now, pay later." It is the way our national debt is growing. The government is modeling this behavior.

JB: Can you describe to some specific areas of your work where the Center has been able to effect change in the consumer sphere on a large scale?

BT: We work to reduce consumption but also to redirect it and this is where we've had some big impact. We work with big institutional buyers ranging from local government agencies, to universities, to churches, to companies who have articulated a set of core values to develop specific preferences for products that align with those values. Those preferences might be environmental, social, or local purchasing from local businesses. There is almost $400 billion spent by local and state governments alone, with hundreds of millions of that now redirected towards companies and products that are environmentally preferable. Whether it is computers, paper, hybrid-electric cars, or non-toxic cleaning products, it sends a clear message to the market. When a corporation changes its behavior to move in a more sustainable direction, there is then a market for it. That, to us, is very powerful. We have helped numerous cities, states, federal agencies and private agencies buy green goods, shifting millions of dollars of buying power. Ultimately, companies listen to big customers.

We've been searching for opportunities to make change along with many other groups—through state and local policy, and through household and life-style changes. We do this with the hope that it begins to add up to a powerful political constituency, a very well organized minority that begins to push and articulate some rule changes, some political changes.

I am also thrilled with the growing number of young people who are pretty savvy about our work and issues. We were assuming our primary base was boomers. However, in focus groups we found a lot of resonance with 20-somethings. There is a feeling among younger people that the boomers have not done it right. Young people on college campuses are on fire with this and don't want to work for a corporate law firm to make tons of money—and not have a life. They want to be part of something different, and they are searching. This has been very exciting. We are developing new programs that speak to this audience as well.

JB: Would you say that there is a spiritual aspect to the work you are doing?

BT: Certainly for me there is, and for many, many people who engage with us. I could not do this work without a contemplative side to my life. We have tried very hard to create the space for people to go deep without requiring any specific inner practice or religious structure.

Many are hungry for a slower pace, for a more peaceful heart, which one can nurture through meditation. If you stop and are quiet, set the wired world aside, you can pay more attention to what you really want and how you want to live, in a human way.

I usually make a radical suggestion that any American can do—take 20 minutes every day in complete silence. Open up to the universe, to something larger than yourself. However one defines it, having a spiritual path, at the minimum, helps us toward healthy judgment and insight, and at its best, offers us wisdom about why we're here and what might be rightful action. For me, it often feels as though the Universe itself is wanting to move in a more loving, healthy direction, and that it needs humans who are open, quiet, and seeking the way. I don't know how to describe this except that I experience it often in my own work.

JB: In the Center's literature there is the theme about taking back your time. It makes me think of Benjamin Franklin's quote: "Time is money." Does the comment speak to a dilemma of our time?

BT: The time issue is connected in part to the global economy and the fact that Americans are working the longest hours in the industrial world right now, with less vacation. This is partly due to material desires for which one needs money—bigger houses, more cars, super-size TV's, multiple everything. Another part is in the nature of the workforce and 24/7 economy where people are expected to work around the clock. Part of it is also a genuine lack of security and a safety net for a growing number of Americans.

If you do not have health insurance, or college tuition paid for, and you're worried about retirement, you have to work to make money to feel safe. All of these things come together to create an explosive work situation. The issue of time and overwork in this country is huge. There is going to be an emerging alignment of a lot of forces around this issue. We just can't keep going this way. I actually see this as a great opportunity—to organize workers for a reduced work week with full benefits. Why not?

JB: Is the Center's work essentially focused on organizing people's conscious participation in the economy?

BT: Organizing people to exercise their economic power is important to social change. In our society, people are able to participate in a lot of different ways. They can participate as citizens. They can participate as consumers, as investors, as people generating their own wealth. They can use their money in ways aligned with their values. People can also just "be the way," living in community, having more fun, ignoring social norms about spending and brands, and convincing others to come along simply because, well, they are smiling more!

JB: The Center has been very effective in its use of the media to create a values-based community. What approach have you taken and how have you accomplished so much in such a short time?

BT: We treat the media and the internet separately. We have been quite adept at telling a story through the media. We have tried to actually create a brand—a look, a feel, an identity—that has emotional resonance with people. With that brand, we tell a story that connects with where people are at right now. Our approach starts there and then opens the doors for them to consider joining with a larger community for a better world and better life. For us, the media has been a tool for outreach. I know it's ironic that we challenge the dominant culture while using some of the dominant culture's tools, but that's what we do! We had a thousand articles about us last year in the media. In the past month or two we have been in *Money* magazine, *People*, *US News and World Report*, CNN, CBS *Market Watch*. I am just doing a commentary for NPR. I think we are successful because we are speaking to people's real concerns—that they're overworked, overspent, worried about the future, worried about their kids, wanting to have something different, wanting the environment to be healthy.

The internet has become the least expensive, easily accessible way to begin creating a new community. At the beginning we didn't know how to be a national group with a local, community-based network. Our most visible focus to date has been an electronic community. We are now aggressively trying to supplement this with an off-line community because it's pretty clear that there are limits to electronic communities. We are trying to make it as informal and lateral as possible.

It is my sense that people across the nation are really hungry to find other people who want to move in the same direction, who want to live the new way, and also push for changes in the larger system. As you do at RSF, we also see many people using their money in positive ways—being charitable or investing in new things, in new ideas. It seems to me that we are in a time when we hear about a lot of darkness all the time in the media, and fear is worked up as a consequence. At the same time, there are quite a lot of people trying to solve problems, and get good work done that we don't hear as much about. It's great that RSF is part of making this good work possible, and I'm hoping that we at the Center can bring a little light to the world as well.

An Interview with Wangari Maathai

Collaboration between organizations is an important challenge for our time. As a social deed it is a path that leverages organizational strengths and creates opportunities for learning. Negotiating agreements, allocating the appropriate human and financial resources, and ensuring that charitable missions remain uncompromised are fundamental to the unfolding of new capacities and relationships. This interview with Wangari Maathai, founder and leader of the Green Belt Movement in Kenya, is the result of one such collaborative moment between RSF Social Finance and the Marion Institute of Marion, Massachusetts. I had the opportunity to interview Professor Maathai while she was in New York to address the United Nations, as well as speak at a Marion Institute event that was celebrating her work.

Since the time of this interview Professor Maathai has been awarded the Nobel Peace Prize for her work in Kenya. She has also received many honors for her work restoring Kenya's environment by leading the Green Belt Movement, which has planted over forty million trees since its inception in 1977 and produced income for hundreds of thousands of people. Equally important, she has devoted her life to furthering the rights of women. Professor Maathi has also received the Africa Prize and the Right Livelihood Award. She is the author of an autobiography, *Unbowed* (2006), *The Challenge for Africa* (2009), and *The Green Belt Movement: Sharing the Approach and the Experience* (2003). She was featured in Kerry Kennedy's book *Speak Truth to Power: Human Rights Defenders Who Are Changing Our World*.

Visionary social entrepreneurship, with all its brilliance and shadows, could not have a more articulate and engaging spokesperson.

This interview was conducted in April 2002.

JB: What made you decide to plant the first trees in your backyard?

WM: On the occasion of World Environment Day, I thought, "Let's mark this day by planting trees." I have always been inspired by people driven by a desire to see life beyond the self and who do things for a common good. To be of service to this common good was one of many original factors that influenced my thinking. This is very powerful in the Green Belt Movement. What we are trying to do is to urge people to look at the whole creation as members of the community of the living—including plants, animals, those we see and those we don't see. On that 5th of June 1977, I decided to plant seven trees to remember seven people who had contributed significantly to the community in which they lived.

JB: Who were the seven people?

WM: These are people I had come to know through civic education, through history. I wanted to encourage people to look back, to remember those that went before us who made those kinds of sacrifices. Consequently, I would tell communities, "Let us plant the trees for anybody in this community whom you remember may have done something for the common good of the community."

JB: Why trees? It could have been roses or other plants.

WM: I think it was a wonderful idea to pick the tree, but it was actually by accident. There are many motivators for this tree planting campaign. One was my serving on the governing committee of the National Council of Women of Kenya. I listened to women speak about the problems they were facing in the 1970s. Remember that the 1970s marked the beginning of what later became the Women's Decade.

The 1970s and 1980s was when women's issues crystallized into a global movement. There was a lot of discussion among women worldwide about the plight of women, the problems they faced, why they faced them, and their historical conditions. In Nairobi, I was one of the privileged women. I had gone to school in the United States. I had returned with a master's degree in biological sciences. I was already working in the University of Nairobi. But, the women who came from organizations based in the rural areas talked about the need for firewood, and for nutritious foods, because people had literally given up food production in order to produce coffee and tea—which they could not eat.

JB: I assume it was an export crop with all the local economic consequences.

WM: It was an export crop. They were left without food and without the capacity to buy food. Because they had cleared the bushes to plant coffee and tea, there were no trees left for the women to get firewood. Also, I had noticed that there was a lot of soil erosion. Because of my scientific training, I very quickly want to know how to solve a problem. As I listened to these women talk of the situation, I thought, "Why not plant trees?" If we planted trees, they would get firewood, fencing materials, and building materials. If they planted fruit trees they would improve nutrition. That was one reason why trees were chosen—of course, to get firewood you could only plant a tree!

Eventually tree planting became a very good symbol of teaching about everything else. It's always easy to tell people, "But, you can at least plant the trees." It's very empowering. It doesn't require much money or too many skills. Consequently, people are able to do it very easily. It is not intimidating.

JB: Is there a mythological or symbolic importance to the trees in addition to the practical qualities? What about the fig tree?

WM: Several generations will worship under the same fig tree. Because it is never cut, the roots must go very deep, most probably all the way down to the underground water level. This is probably why wherever there was a fig tree there was usually a spring or a little stream. So, our people associated fig trees with water. I think that what the tree's roots do is break the underground rock and allow water to gush out. It's really wonderful—like bringing the richness of the soil out for the people. Maybe this is something that was revealed to the ancient people. But our people did not write down a lot of this wisdom.

JB: This happens in many oral traditions.

WM: Oral traditions have the disadvantage that they can easily be lost. But there is a lot of wisdom in them. They did not say, "Do not cut these trees because they bring underground water to the surface." Instead, they said, "Do not cut these trees because they are trees of God." The original wisdom and inspiration was translated into activities and rituals that eventually become part of the culture. Over time people forget how the inspiration came and it just becomes a routine.

JB: How did this ritual of planting your seven trees transform into a whole social movement?

WM: When we started, we were not planning a movement. A movement came almost by chance. We were responding to the need of the women for firewood, and to reduce soil erosion. I remember when we first went to the nursery. Everybody wanted to have a tree. That surprised me, because I thought people were not keen to plant trees. What I discovered later is that the government tree nurseries were very far from the people—hence the need for local tree nurseries. The second thing we discovered was that planting trees was made to appear like a profession. Ordinary illiterate people did not see that they could do it without the direction of a forester. Third, there was no tradition of deliberately planting trees, because historically there was abundant wood, no commercial agriculture, and very low population density.

JB: It probably seemed that there would always be enough.

WM: There was always enough until later when commercial agriculture, clearcutting, and large farms were introduced. The colonialists [Kenya was a British colony from late in the nineteenth century until its independence in 1963—*ed.*] did not want to see a tree on the land because trees were like an enemy of the tractor. They deliberately cleared thousands of acres of indigenous forest to replace it with imported trees like evergreens and eucalyptus. This was very typical of the British. Wherever they went they brought everything with them. In East Africa, the eucalyptus and pines became very economically productive trees. The new settlers needed a lot of fast-growing trees to provide the wood for the steam engines. A lot of destruction was done during this time of new settlements. There was no time for the natural regeneration to take place anymore. It was not even being given a chance; therefore, we had to start planting. Until then, God was always planting trees for the people. But the time had come when God needed a little help.

JB: You began as an environmentalist reclaiming land and planting trees to meet the needs of the people. But this activity also has a political side. When did this aspect become apparent?

WM: When I was at the University of Nairobi, I thought that my job was just to teach and to promote the cause of women. I did not think that what I was doing had anything to do with politics. Even when we started planting trees, I did not see the role of politics in what we were doing. Later we decided to give civic and environmental education to the communities we were working with so that they would see why they, rather than the government, should be planting trees and preventing soil erosion on their farms, and protecting the local species of plants and food crops.

That was when I first confronted politics. That's when I first was prevented from holding such meetings without a license. I wanted to know why I needed a license to meet my fellow Kenyans. That was, for me, an encounter with the oppressive and authoritarian system of governance that we had. The new independent government was set up to control people, to control the information they get, to make sure that they remain very fearful of the government, so they do not question it. The more I learned about this system, the more I challenged it, the more I realized that even a simple thing like planting trees can become political.

If I were just going around planting trees and telling people to plant trees, nobody would bother me. But the minute I said, "I passed through the forest and saw that some trees in the forest have been cut. Who has cut them?" That's when the problem started, because leaders were misusing their positions to log illegally for private benefit. It did not make sense to me that we should be telling women to plant and protect trees, while government agents were busy cutting other trees. In trying to stop that cutting—that's when politics came in. They did not want to be exposed because they were enriching themselves with these natural resources. What amazes me is that they don't care about the damage they cause. They will harvest trees in a watershed area even though they know they are going to interfere with the water flow, disturb the availability of water downstream, and hasten soil erosion.

Of course, one just can't tell women, "Let us stop soil erosion." One wants to stop what is causing soil erosion, namely deforestation. That's when it really became a fight. In trying to help communities, one is also trying to protect them from governance that really doesn't support them, because it is very destructive to the environment.

JB: What is the role of men in all of this? Where are they?

WM: To answer your question, one needs to revisit the history of Africa and its colonization. Understand that when one enters into a country to colonize, one has to demobilize the men because it is the men who will be the first to oppose the invaders. One way they did this was to institutionalize a lot of the traditional roles of men. For example, in East Africa, men were responsible for providing security to the community.

When the colonists brought in an army and police, they told every man to join—he was trained, given a uniform, and swore an oath of allegiance to the colonial government. This took a lot of men away from the community to provide the kind of security the colonial government wanted. Those not in the army or the police were just sitting down doing nothing because it was no longer their business to provide security. In fact, if they tried, they'd be arrested.

The second way in which many men were immobilized was the creation of jobs. The colonialists needed labor, so the bosses came up with a very ingenious system of "hat taxes," a tax on every adult male. One had to pay the tax with money—a coin. Nobody had used money like that before. My community was using sheep and goats as the basis of exchange, whether buying land or paying dowry, they had a value. The colonial settlers said, "I don't want any goats. I want a coin. I have the coins. You have to go to work for me to get the coins and pay your taxes." Men then had to move from their communities to go and look for jobs on farms or in urban centers. Once men moved from their communities they could no longer stay with their families, organize, or resist. The net result of this was that the women were left in their communities.

It's also true, especially in eastern Africa, that women do a lot of work in the field. Traditionally men looked after livestock, provided security, broke the ground, left for trade or to war. The role of women was to work on the land, produce food crops, and take care of their families. That legacy has continued to this day.

These days there is such high unemployment that we can no longer absorb men into the army, police, white collar jobs, even in the blue collar jobs. There are a lot of excess males just doing nothing except engaging in self-destructive activities. This is a shame and needs to be addressed. It has its root in the colonial period.

We have come to accept as a norm that the men will go away to work and the women will stay home. This situation has greatly contributed to the spread of AIDS, which first struck in the urban centers. It was taken to the villages by men who live in these centers and every so often return to the rural areas. The poor women in the rural areas have become victims of a disease that was actually brought to them by husbands who are forced to live away from them.

JB: You made a transition from biological sciences into the environmental movement only to discover that environmental issues are all-encompassing in terms of economics, politics, culture, and spirit. When did you notice that in the transition you had become a leader of a movement?

WM: When I started planting trees it was almost like entering an unknown sphere. I gradually discovered the world in that sphere, and discovered the linkages between different spheres. However things are easier said than done. For example, you begin to see that God is not exactly the way He was presented in high school or in church as an old man with a white beard. Life is so mysterious that I do not really understand it. I only know I am a participant. I am just like a drop and this life span of mine is short. If I'm only a drop, I want to be a full and effective drop. I have become not more religious, but more spiritual. I have discovered my relationship with a much bigger human community than I used to see. I see myself as a member of the living community of plants, animals, of everything that lives. I have a lot of humility now because of what I have come to understand.

Based on the Bible, I was taught that there is a hierarchy and that human beings are at the top of the hierarchy. However, that is man's interpretation. Sometimes I think that man was created on Saturday because he couldn't live without the creation that preceded him. If God had created man on Monday, he would have been dead on Tuesday, because he couldn't survive! This should really humble us. We are endowed with a consciousness that is higher than the consciousness of other members—we are aware of ourselves and others, and we try very hard to understand. With this understanding, my environmentalism takes on a completely different meaning. My conscience tells me to complete my evolutionary piece because I am playing a part in a long process. Environmentalism then takes on a very, very deep spiritual meaning that has nothing to do with where God is and whether I will go there to live with Him or whether when I die that's the end of me as me. Sometimes I wish I had understood this much earlier, so that I could have had time to do more.

JB: Is it your hope that through the Green Belt Movement, others begin to experience their own spirituality as well?

WM: Yes. In fact, that's one of the reasons why I have tried to partner with religious leaders in civic and environmental education seminars. Our clergy needs to understand much, much better the relationship between spirituality, religion, and the environment. We live on a continent where there are a lot of problems—poverty, diseases, and ignorance. I am saddened when people are persuaded to believe that it's okay to be in the state that they are, that maybe they cannot do anything about it because they should accept what God has given. People *can* plant trees, provide themselves with shade, fruit, and clean drinking water. They can feed themselves and jump up and down for joy because they are healthy. Like the Garden of Eden, one should be able to just stretch out a hand and pick a fruit from the tree. We should believe in plenty. That's the way it is intended.

JB: But this will arise from both developing consciousness and work.

WM: We have to do the work. That's what many people need to appreciate. You have to do the work. That is why the Bible says you will eat the fruits of your labor. That means we should not accept greed. We should not accept corruption. We should not accept injustices. We should not accept inequalities. This is why human rights issues are so important to me—to respect human beings with dignity. But human beings must also realize that it is they who must wake up and go to the river and drink of the water. The water will not come to them.

Epilogue

Money Weighs and Means

ONE COULD ARGUE that our perception determines how we value money, what meaning it has for us in the hierarchy of our experience. If this is the case, it becomes easier to understand how the appearance of value, and the assumed monetary measure attached to that value, can rise and fall so quickly. The state of one's perception is as dependent on inner security and trust as our bank accounts and the value of the dollar are on the security of governmental guarantee. So, for better or worse, money is tethered to that aspect of our character which senses whether the exercise of trust is valid and safe. The challenge of our time is that the money messages received through that sense—the economic story, the disparity between wealth and poverty, and the easy and illusory access to debt—have been mixed, confusing, and for some, disempowering. Thus the genius of money, what good wealth has done in the world, is inseparable from the more adumbrated realities of race, class, and gender.

This complex reality was already weighing on the American consciousness in the mid-nineteenth century. Ralph Waldo Emerson, wrote his essay "Wealth" (Section III, *Conduct of Life*, 1860), in the midst of a rising tide of civil activism focused on the separate matters of race, class and gender. Abolitionists fought to eliminate slavery culminating with the Emancipation Proclamation of 1862. The suffrage movement for women's equality had its beginnings with the Seneca Falls Convention of 1848, the same year that the worker's movements received their class-based philosophical roots in the work of Marx and Engels with the publication of the *Communist Manifesto*.

Though he was engaged in and advocated for such rights, Emerson primarily addressed spiritual, moral, and ethical issues of wealth as a basis for personal transformation or transcendence. One particular reference is to the perception of value and the weight of money as an indicator of cultural change:

> Money is representative, and follows the nature and fortunes of the owner. The coin is a delicate meter of civil, social, and moral changes. The farmer is covetous of his dollar, and with reason. It is no waif to him. He knows how many strokes of labor it represents. His bones ache with the day's work that earned it. He knows how much land it represents;— how much rain, frost, and sunshine. He knows that, in the dollar, he gives you so much discretion and patience, so much hoeing and threshing. Try to lift his dollar; you must lift all that weight. In the city, where money follows the skit of a pen, or a lucky rise in exchange, it comes to be looked at as light. I wish the farmer held it dearer, and would spend it only for real bread; force for force.
>
> The farmer's dollar is heavy, and the clerk's is light and nimble; leaps out of his pocket; jumps on to cards and farotables; but still more curious is its susceptibility to metaphysical changes. It is the finest barometer of social storms, and announces revolutions.

Emerson's penetrating perception led him to identify in money the constellation of inner experience and outer actions, and that the value of money is in some ways the handmaiden of all the forces at work in culture. Though he did not say it directly, money is, among all its other functions, an expression of evolution of human consciousness. While Emerson witnessed all of this civil change arising, an understanding and articulation of how these changes would so intertwine in the economic system of the modern industrial West had yet to surface.

In some ways it is just emerging at the dawn of the twenty-first century, though our global consciousness has brought us an ever-present awareness of the interdependence and, in many cases, painful confluences of these many threads. The bodies of knowledge focused on race, class, and gender as issues unto themselves have grown exponentially since Emerson's time. The same cannot be said for our understanding of money. It has remained a challenging and taboo topic.

We are being forced by economic crisis to look at the deeper issues of money—its shadows, light, power, and its evanescence. It is a great bellwether of the state of our consciousness. It is time to look at the hard issues, especially money, in a new way that incorporates spirit and social values. If anything has been made clear, it is that when money is disconnected from real economic activity and human productivity, it too easily becomes an end unto itself. Financial transactions then become impenetrable, opaque, and unaccountable in the true sense of the words. When money is an end rather than a means, transparency is an enemy, trust a victim. Money has become so abstract it can no longer be weighed, though it weighs on us, and each of us, with our credits and debits, lives within its meaning.

Money reflects the architecture of human experience—both our inner and outer spaces. Architecture, especially buildings, very much conditions our experience of space, and, the transition from outside to inside, the peristyles, portals, and sanctuary, the light and darkness. The ancient Greek temple is an illuminating example. Usually devoted to a particular god, each temple also had a treasury at its center, the inner sanctum, the protected space. This is religion—mythic beliefs and their statuary embodiments—co-housed with sacrificial material offerings, mostly gold and other precious goods. If one can accept this structure also as metaphor for personal experience—that we house within us our own treasury of gifts and offerings which we protect and use as resource at the same time—then one can see how money, as we have come to know it in modern times, is still connected to each person's inner sanctum within the temple of individuality. We make our own walls to protect and rules to govern. However, we know only too well from daily experience how money connects us to the outer world of materials, relationships, and values. We need only tap into our sense of integrity to see how connected to or disconnected from our deepest values our behaviors around money are.

Collectively, the essays and interviews included here have pointed to the possibility of self-transformation as a starting point for changing ourselves, our local community and eventually the financial system. They also indicated what is wrong with our current system. Any invention of the mind (in this case money and debt) that is managed in order to dehumanize its users needs a new set of ethical practices that might take a cue from the ancient temples and the origins of money in Western civilization. There can be a quality of offering in and through every financial transaction. Each of us can become more conscious of the intentions in financial behavior, or more aware of the work and economic efforts of others to make the transactions possible at all. But first I, and I would invite the reader, to wake up to the pain and inequity that have grown within the system even as I have participated willingly, if not wisely, in it.

In the ancient temples, the priest class held the spiritual powers of initiation, and thus was perceived to hold the wisdom to govern the treasury well. That has changed in the modern era. Each of us now has the capacity to initiate ourselves, to develop our own consciousness. Along with this capacity, the wisdom to be a "treasurer" and economic citizen needs to develop. We can no longer afford to cede that capacity to those operating in the old consciousness of "priesthood." This collection of essays and interviews is an exploration of the origins and expressions of this transformed consciousness through the window of money and financial transactions. The essays look at cultural artifacts, art, events and research as indicators of that consciousness. The interviews provide insights into the capacity for self-transformation in the economic and money realms, to demonstrate and practice the integration of values, intuition (deep inner practices) with outer action.

The research and writing of these essays has also been a journey for me, a path of inquiry and insight into an arena of the personal and cultural life of money that has remained taboo. If this book lifts the veil of this taboo, even a little bit, and creates permission and fuel for each and every reader to engage in a similar process, as joyous and painful as that will be, much will have been accomplished. If the essays and interviews become a source of conversation, for shared perspectives, for honest reflections, a new sense of community may emerge. With good faith, hope, and love, heretofore unspoken assumptions about wealth, money, and power, can find a living and transparent place in the formation of social life. Sadly, it is often the unspoken assumptions that play in the shadows of our financial lives and thus add a quiet violence to our transactional activity—working in groups and organizations, and even in the agreements we make with ourselves.

Spirit has everything to do with money, just as money has everything to do with our daily lives. To the degree that we can bring out the elements of ritual, of sacrifice and gain, of a living picture of stewardship rather than materialistic ownership in our financial transactions, we will change the world through a sense of collaboration rather than competition, interdependence rather than self-interest, and a sense for real peace in our economic lives.